The Magic of Being the Claus

The *Magic* of Being the *Claus*

Chuck Hubbell

Ourlink
PRINT & MEDIA

The Magic of Being the Claus

1603 Capitol Ave., Suite 310 Cheyenne, Wyoming USA 82001
1-888-980-6523 | admin@urlinkpublishing.com

URLink Print and Media is committed to excellence in the publishing industry.

Book design copyright © 2019 by URLink Print and Media. All rights reserved.

Published in the United States of America
ISBN 978-1-64367-324-0 (Paperback)
ISBN 978-1-64367-323-3 (Digital)
28.03.19

INTRODUCTION

This book is about a journey. A journey of creating magic with children. It sheds light on why creating magic for children is important. It is about a journey into the realm of children whose innocence is taken from them far too soon. It is about smiles and laughter and secrets and perhaps a little magic that results in believing. Believing for a moment longer or if we are lucky, another year. Or if we really believe perhaps that magic can last a lifetime.

But this story is about so much more. It is about what children gave me as I evolved into being a Santa Claus. It is about how I became a much better person. It is a story about how I gained insight and understanding in the power of believing when believing seems impossible.

This story has no specific location or time as it could be anywhere in small town America during anytime of the twenty first century. The names were changed to give that; anywhere, anytime feel to the story but the events and the Magic are real.

ACKNOWLEDGEMENTS

It is with extreme humility that I acknowledge the following people and organizations for their believing in me.

First on the list is my wife, Drema, who has endured countless hours of hearing about the Claus and his antics. Also she was always there when I needed a shoulder to lean on. Although she has never been Mrs. Claus, She has always been Mrs. Chuck and I could not be prouder. She was responsible for all the details that helped me become the best Claus I could be.

Cindy Hanzes for providing interpretation for the hearing impaired. Vicki McWilliams who earned her Master's degree in Elfology. Next on my list is my friend and editor, Chuck Motycka who was very dedicated in giving of his valuable time and expertise to help move a concept about the Claus and Magic for children as portrayed in a very rough draft into a polished book. I am eternally grateful. My friend Gerry Browell has been the inspiration to continue the magic. Nancy Henry also deserves and needs special mention as editing skill and her expertise in promotion and public relations pointed me in the right direction. Mary Dreliszak, whose Blog on people who inspire, motivated me to continue and inspire.

Countless organizations and people need to be acknowledged and thanked. But I am afraid that since there are so many, I could possibly leave one out. One would be too many. Be sure however I am extremely grateful to all the stores and groups and day care providers and individuals that let me create magic with children of all ages. My life has been enhanced greatly.

No acknowledgement would be complete without mentioning the City of Connellsville, The Downtown Revitalization Committee,

The Connellsville Planning Commission, The Chamber of Commerce and The Fayette County Cultural Trust, The Connellsville Canteen and Armstrong My Wire cable company. However, my deepest and most sincere thanks is reserved for The Connellsville Rotary Club. For years their financial contributions have allowed me to provide meaningful gifts for special needs children of the community. It is because of this wonderful organization that, I believe in the magic.

DEDICATION

For people of all ages,
Believing in the Magic
Of Christmas

CONTENTS

A JOURNEY OF A THOUSAND MILES BEGINS WITH THE FIRST STEP

Chinese Proverb

The journey began somewhere between you have two weeks to complete this assignment, and this is going to take forever, I'll never get it finished. Mr. Michael Hanson, my high school speech teacher, had given the class an assignment that would change my life forever. Because of this assignment I began to learn how to be comfortable in standing before a group and saying a few words. I learned to use my vocal cords to speak, to teach, and to help others believe. I learned the power of having thoughts move from my brain to my mouth by using my vocal cords in a coordinated manner.

The assignment was to memorize a poem and present that selection to the class "dramatically". The stakes were high. This assignment would count for 1/3 of our semester grade. But a poor grade was not my greatest fear. Speaking in public terrified me, I wasn't even comfortable speaking privately so I believed that I was doomed to fail. I was the premier wallflower afraid to speak, much less to speak my mind. I had been laughed at more than once in my life and I was sure that this would be just one more time I would receive my share of public humiliation. Since I had attended several schools, I was always the new kid. As the new kid I was bullied everywhere I went. But, that story is best left for the Dr. Phil television show.

I had so many doubts about the whole thing… What was I going to do? I had always liked that story or whatever it was about Santa Claus that I had heard as a kid. Would that work…? What was it called again…? Since this was way before the instant access of the internet, how was I to get the words...? Did my mother or younger siblings have the story somewhere...? How could I possibly ever remember the lines in sequence...? Could I learn the cadence and rhythm and the timing? What if I got confused and spoke about sugar plums in a bowl full of jelly? What if I got stage fright and just stood there, not saying anything? What if...?

The class and I endured renditions of "Gunga Din"; "The Charge of the Light Brigade"; "The Road Not Taken"; and "Casey at the Bat"; each classmate received polite, nervous applause from those yet to present as we all mentally rehearsed our own presentations over and over. Then it was my turn.

As my name was called, I knew I had to force myself to stand up straight, keep my knees from buckling, walk to the front of the room, present my poem and run back to my chair as soon as I could. Somehow I made it to the front of the room. Now was the time to speak, but I uttered not a sound. What once seemed like an eternity, quickly passed. All of the sudden "'Twas the night before Christmas and all through the house, not a creature was stirring, not even a mouse," burst forth from my mouth. Several people smiling and no one booing as I spoke gave me the incentive to proceed. And proceed I did. I delivered all the words in the correct sequence and with a sense of cadence and rhythm I had not known before. I closed my eyes when I finished. I heard noise that sounded like clapping, and when I re-opened them I saw that the entire class clapping. I had never experienced applause before, and it felt good.

Most of us had to memorize things like the preamble to the Constitution of the United States and the Gettysburg Address in high school. But I also memorized the classic poem that creates the current image of Santa Claus to our world today. The pictures and other depictions of Santa seem all to be based on the image created by Clement C. Moore. At that time I had no idea what impact this 500 plus word poem would have on my future life.

Two marriages, two children, six grand-children, and forty four years later, I can still recite that classic poem "dramatically" in much the same way I did so long ago. Like the song you can't get out of your head, that great poem is with me all the time. It comes to me especially at Christmas when the Icon of Santa appears everywhere. I have even parodied the poem several times, to help deal with a few situations I was facing.

I had never given much thought to being that Santa guy, but for some reason I started to perfect the technique of saying "HO HO HO". A few years ago, I happened to need something from the same room where the Downtown Christmas Committee was conducting an emergency meeting to find a new Santa. Due to illness the current black booted, red coated, fake bearded, occupant of the job was no longer available. I asked for permission to retrieve my needed item and then intended to leave. Fate had other intentions. While I had my head in the closet, one of my friends on the committee asked me to say "ho ho ho". My guess was… that since I had throughout my life gained weight, that I was unable to keep off, I was once again in for a humiliation fat shot. Well I always thought that if you are to go down, you should go down swinging.

So, from down deep in my diaphragm I brought forth a resounding "HO HO HO!" I was going to show them alright. They might have made fun of me for being large, well extra-large, or maybe 2X large. Ok I'm 4 inches too short for my weight, but I wasn't about to let anyone ridicule the way I uttered those three famous words. I said "HO HO HO!" like I knew what I was doing. Someone said "He will be perfect." Then the same person asked if I had ever played Santa before. My instincts yelled watch out, here it comes. I confessed to the meeting participants that I was asked once to be Santa and that I even tried on the suit they had. I had to also admit that I was greatly embarrassed because the Santa suit was too small.

She said, I would be using the Chamber's suit if it fit me. If the suit did not fit, they would try to get someone else. I was thinking, if it didn't fit, I wouldn't even consider it (apologies to Johnny Cochran). I was urged to go to the Chamber office to see if the suit fit. Sounded like my way out. The next day I went to try on the Chamber's suit. All the while I was thinking I'll soon be able to dash away, dash away, far from here. Wrong! The suit fit!

Soon I was dressed all in red fur, from my head to my foot. The good news–I wasn't covered in ashes and soot. My new Preoccupation

-- how am I going to get out of this? It was less than two weeks until the Santa was needed. Temporarily trapped, I asked "what was expected of Santa?" Foolish question...

The answer was deceptively simple. Santa would ride to a pavilion in the city park on the back of a buckboard wagon driven by two horses, sit on Santa's throne, ask the children what they wanted for Christmas, give them each a candy cane, and make time to have their photo taken. Then Santa would invite the kids to participate in the fun stuff, such as having their faces painted, decorating their very own Christmas cookies, or getting their own balloon animal made by a clown.

THE CLAUS 1.0

Since it wasn't a miniature sleigh with eight tiny reindeer, it was suggested that I mount the buckboard from the back. That way, I could stand and wave to the kids. There was an issue or two with this horse drawn wagon of olden days. The buckboard bed was higher than I could stretch my legs even in my younger days when I ran track in high school. And the driver had left the stepstool at home. I recalled all those television shows and movies where I had seen someone take their position on the buckboard. They all made it look soooo easy… It isn't. I turned and jumped, praying I wouldn't hurt myself or worse fall. I didn't fall, I was aboard onto my backside then to my knees to my feet and the coursers they flew. I now stood ready and waiting… at that same moment in time, the mare started to show the impatience of a cat on a hot tin roof. When she moved, I lost my footing nearly cascading off the rear of the buckboard. As I caught my balance I informed the two people who were there, that I was a highly trained professional and they were not to try this maneuver at home. Then I made an executive decision. I'm not standing.

Now, it was time for the parade to move forward to all the waiting children… All… none of them… I had risked life and limb and my dignity to mount a buckboard, keep my balance, and climb over the seat, smile and wave to… no one.

I was able to dismount (I think that is the correct term) more gracefully and move to the throne in the pavilion and wait. The temperature was the lowest it had been all winter. It was cold. Did I mention, that it was cold? Bone numbing, turn every limb on your body to icicles, cold. I was ready to go home to the warmth of my hearth and wife. Who ever thought this was going to be a good idea?

Is it over yet? I have never been so miserable in all my life. Santa! Bah Humbug! Never, never again in my life.

The families that had planned to come to the park, have their turn to ride on the buckboard, visit with Santa, have their faces painted, watch the clown twist balloons into animal shapes, sip the hot chocolate and decorate their own cookies, were obviously going to wait until the day got warmer.

It didn't. It was over an hour before the first brave family with a 6 month old very bundled up baby ventured out for the festivities of the day. It could have been a Cabbage Patch Doll for all I knew. No buck board ride for them. No face painting. No balloon animals. No hot chocolate. No cookies. Take the picture with Santa and go home.

My preparations for the day included a visit to the internet and a Google search for "How to be a good Santa." The top piece of information I gleaned from that trip on the information superhighway was try to know the children's names before they came to sit on your lap. In addition Santa must know the names of the Reindeer in order, and of course, Rudolph. Then there is the riddle about what is the name of the tenth reindeer --- "Olive" as in, "ALL OF" the other reindeer.

Some brave people brought their dog for a photo with Santa. I love dogs but spending a couple of hours on the coldest day of the year for a photo with a dog... boy, life for me had dropped to a very low point. So far I only had to know Max and the name of a six month old baby, I think... whose name I immediately forgot.

MAGIC

Then the magic happened. Her name was Gabriella. She looked to be 9 or 10. She was hiding behind the tree. Santa's elves had worked hard to find out the names of the few children visiting Santa. By now they were so bored that they had time to find out that the shy girl behind the tree believed in the Easter Bunny, and the Tooth Fairy, but not Santa; he was for little children. No Santa!? Oh, my gosh, I've always loved a challenge. I was going to get her to talk to me, Oh, by gosh, by golly. By a magical process known only to Santa her name was now tucked into Santa's brain and on his lips.

In the twinkling of his eye, Santa said "Gabriella, is that you?" With a response that would have made Elvis jealous, she shrieked, "Oh! Mommy he knows my name!!!" Instantly the magic happened. She came to me, sat on my lap, looked at me and told me all she wanted for Christmas. She had her photo taken, drank hot chocolate, and ate her candy cane. Then she came back, sat down again and told me more. Since there were no other children waiting, Santa had the time to listen. She was so wide-eyed with excitement. Her entire demeanor changed. She became the magic. She now believed in the Easter Bunny, the Tooth Fairy and Santa Claus again. All of the elves helping me that day were amazed at her turn around.

Almost everyone remarked how special that moment was. As Santa, I was completely overwhelmed with that moment. The magic came to me that day as well. I can do "this" I thought. And do "this" I did. Later, that day many other children came to see Santa and enjoy the festivities waiting for them that cold day. But they were not able to re-create the magic. With the big day over, it was time for the big guy to return the suit. Santa is in the limelight just once a year. But,

19

I learned for at least one day or perhaps one month of the year, I could create magic. But I know to be good, real magic requires more preparation than two weeks. I was told by the organizers that I was the best Santa they had seen. How many had they seen?

I was asked if the situation presented itself next year, did I want to be the Claus. Yes, was my quick and sure reply. I have always been a perfectionist. So I pondered, how do you do something that countless millions have done and want – and expect–to be as good as or better than those who came before? How do you prepare? How do you create magic? What can it be like to "be" the Claus? I was told I had been the best... But what did that mean? What would I change to become a better Claus?

I have observed many a "Santa" in action and have learned from both the worst and the best, for the perfection of the craft. Some people think you can become Santa by putting on a red suit and a fake beard. I think that is like thinking you can drive a NASCAR because you drive fast on the interstate.

The Chamber provided Santa suit came with a hat that was well worn and two sizes too small. The entire suit has aging issues. I later discovered it was at least 15 years old. I guess when it is used once a year, 15 years of wear seemed brand new to somebody. My wife didn't think so. There were issues with the seams coming apart, and she had to stitch with dental floss to keep them together. The clothes were all tarnished with ashes and soot. Well, if I am going to be the Claus, maybe having my own suit would be in order. I figure it is like finally deciding to buy a tuxedo. But I really believe the Santa suit will get more use, and I'm sure I can find one in my size.

The beard the chamber had provided for my first time had been used before. It was so bad that on the night before my first appearance I knew that I had to get a new one. I threw the disgusting thing down to the ground. I swear it moved. Fake beards look well... fake. That fake beard was nasty. It was yellow next to my skin. And I resented having to inhale whatever cancer causing agents were floating in the synthetic hair. But why use a fake beard? Why not have a real beard for future appearances?

I wondered how long it would take for me to sport a beard that would look as real as Santa's should look. I asked other real bearded Santas how long it took to grow the beard. "Six to nine months... Better start by July 1st," They advised. I decided that in the future I was going to be better prepared. I had never grown a beard as long as the one I anticipated I would need to be a convincing Santa. Acting on faith – I had not officially been asked to be Santa again -- I started growing the beard on July 1st. The itching only lasted a week. The beard prompted all sorts of discussion... hope it looks OK. I don't even know if I am going to be asked to be the Claus more than one time.

The magician's code is made up of two tenants: never perform the magic trick twice to the same audience and never tell the audience how the trick is performed. Christmas Magic with Santa is never the same. It can happen at the most unexpected time. And it usually happens only once. It is that WOW factor moment. It can happen more than once, but you can't plan on it ever happening.

By September 1st, I was officially asked if I wanted to once again create some magic being the Claus. It was like getting my second bicycle. Yes, I would be "The Claus." (My, un-official nickname for myself) I would be honored. I guess once you put on the suit some magic appears from somewhere. And once you decide you can be the right Jolly Old Elf, the magic is solidified.

Representatives from the Downtown Christmas Experience Committee asked me to do a return engagement as Santa. But this year we were going to be inside–no buckboard, no horses, no clown, no balloons twisted into animal shapes. It would be just the children and the Claus. It was to be downtown... in a store with people coming to the store as a destination. It was to be part of the whole downtown Christmas Experience. WOW, I'm impressed. It wasn't really the same, but why quibble? It was time to get serious. Perfect the look by using the Chamber's suit again but this time with a real beard.

I was sure there was some stuff one could use to make the real beard white. Since I live in a small town, I worried about finding magical whitener. Before the gig, I happened to be in a much bigger city and made it my business to go to a store that offered theatre make-up and other stuff. I had no idea what to ask for, so I told my story in far greater detail than was necessary. In 2.1 seconds the proprietor handed me a jar of stuff and wisely cautioned me not to "use the brush that comes in the bottle, use a toothbrush instead." Thinking, I didn't want to whiten my teeth, but… I held my tongue. I was just glad to get the stuff, whatever it was.

LIFE AS THE CLAUS
OR NOT SO MUCH...

My wife and I went to a party in November and the theme was a luau. Great! Santa, "The Claus," was going to a luau! I put on my best Hawaiian shirt, whitened my real beard, put on a wig, sunglasses, shorts, sandals and my new best Santa hat. It was easy to learn that children of all ages can create in their own minds the magic of days gone by... by just by being near Santa. People sat on my lap and danced with me. The DJ was very tickled with my perfected bellowing of "HO HO HO!" We did the Limbo and Santa led a snake dance throughout the room. I guess you can have a lot of fun when you are in costume. Several people confessed to being nice–and I'm sure they were sincere–but the ones confessing to being naughty were the funniest. I told them to call me, but none ever did.

We went to three other Christmas parties armed with a white beard and a hardy "HO HO HO, HO HO HO, HO HO HO!!!" Most people were amused and magic was created as they tried to guess, "is he or isn't he?" It was wonderful that people even suspected he might be... no he can't be... but he sure looks and sounds like Santa "HO HO HO!!!"

On another occasion we were driving in the vicinity of the City of Western Power, a City that takes its security very seriously. We were near the hub of constant motorcades and Secret Service details and the largest collection of huge black SUVs in the world. I was driving in the middle lane of a three-lane highway my beard whitened, red shirt, wig, sunglasses and my great new Santa hat. When, in the next lane there arose such a clatter, I immediately glanced to my left to see what was the matter. When what to my wondering eyes should appear, but a big black SUV, moving closer I feared. Suddenly it crossed in front of my Jeep sleigh into my lane and then into the next one over. The vehicle slowed and down came its rear window. The thought crossed my mind that something could happen here, and it could be bad.

All of the sudden a young boy waved and waved. It was then we knew we had nothing to fear. This child saw the magic in a car next to him. He spoke not a word, but waved with both hands and smiled once again from ear to ear. He was glad to be wished a Happy Christmas from the Claus in a blue Jeep. His dad gave a wave and honked on his horn and to his team gave a whistle as he drove out of sight. And they were gone. Magic!

It must be the whitened real beard that helps with the magic. For that weekend the whitened beard was part of the all-day attire. From then on, whenever shopping was on the agenda, Santa was sure to have his beard whitened. People talked to me, several children asked if my reindeer were outside. Seeing children in a store watching me from the corner of their eyes, would motivate me to move a couple of aisles away and let escape a hearty "HO HO HO!" It was magic to hear the reactions. If someone stopped to watch me pick up something the big guy would say, "Since we ran out of these at the North Pole, here is where we come to get some." "HO HO HO, HO HO HO!"

One day Santa went into a candy store here in town that sold handmade chocolate delights and all the customers and candy makers felt the magic of Santa in plain clothes in the store. Letting the people outside know that was the place to shop for my Chocolate candy needs. "HO HO HO!" The "HO HO HOs!!!" were becoming more frequent and better sounding. In the days leading up to Christmas, people were asking themselves if the man in the white beard was really Santa. More magic was created for the adults who seemed to be inquiring the most. It was difficult not to reply with a twinkle in my eyes. I let them draw their own conclusions.

On an evening trip to the local Wal-Mart, I encountered a group of cheerleaders ringing the bell for Salvation Army. As I approached them I reached down and began bellowing of "HO HO HO!!!" They shouted out with glee in seeing The Claus and hearing his signature "HO HO HO, HO HO HO!!!" They yelled to all their friends, "Come here and see Santa," It was very important that they didn't destroy the "reality" of Santa for the younger children. They took my picture. With all the cell phone cameras available, it would be extremely difficult to guess how many people took a picture of me as "The Claus" that night and throughout the season. Magic! "HO HO HO, HO HO HO, HO HO HO!" Magic!

THE CLAUS 2.0

Well, the big day finally arrived. The transition into being "The Claus." was in full swing. Since the show must go on, Santa Kicked into performance mode, and Santa is planning to have a really good time. "HO HO HO, HO HO HO, HO HO HO!!!"

The Chamber's suit was mine for another day but usable only after my wife had to spent another evening to sew up the new seam flaws. The beard was "whitened." The wig and hat were in place and I was ready. Arriving at the designated building, I encountered my nemesis "You're a mean one, Mr. Grinch" and his newly recruited "helper", Cindy Lu Who. It seemed that Cindy Lu Who, had moved to the dark side. Until she displayed her one pointed ear and winked, these were the qualifications in her mind that automatically elevated her to "ELFit" or North Pole speak for "Elf in training." There we were, The Grinch, Cindy Lu Who, my seven year old "ELF in training" and myself. We entered the building and moved to Santa's throne. I had never conducted the on the job training with a new ELF before. The ELF union had their own apprenticeship program and in the past had been super-efficient.

Not having seen her resume made it difficult to determine her experience level, so she was assigned some simple ELF tasks. She was to hand out the candy canes to each child. When she needed something different to do, she went outside and rang the jingle bells and waved to the passers-by. Many people honked at her, but in reality they were honking at the adult female ELF as she waved. Sometimes, the Claus would get out of the big chair and go outside to wave at the passers-by. Horns honked, and most people waved back. There were new additions to the naughty list that day as a few

26

teens indicated to Santa that he was number one in their book by displaying their middle finger. Several people yelled out how nice they had been this past year as they drove by.

Many children sat in Santa's lap that day, and the older Elves did an excellent job. Cindy Lu Who was a wide-eyed child who hung on my every word. She accepted with the utmost faith that everything Santa said was true. I had to be very careful to stay in character with her all day. Yes, she was there all day as her mother was the photographer for the children. It was necessary to help her balance the idea that Santa's Elves didn't complain about the cold with the need for her to wear a coat when she was outside. She finally agreed to wear a coat and not complain. During the day Cindy Lu Who ate too many of the candy canes, the reason she was rolling on a super sugar high. Sugar affected her imagination and stimulated her non-stop vocal cords.

Before each child made it up to the big chair, the un-scrolling and careful examination of "Santa's Top Secret Naughty or Nice List" made quite an impression. One young boy used his future lawyer skills to challenge my pronouncement that he was now on the naughty list. After a fair presentation of his case, he won removal from the "NAUGHTY" list and secured a place on the "NICE" side. Magic! Then the magic happened again! Six year old Tiffany was telling her five year old sister Jenny "that's the real SANTA, did you hear him laugh?" "HO HO HO, HO HO HO, HO HO HO!!!"

Near the end of the day two boys came into the store. The store instantly filled with silence. It was the look on their faces that gave them away. There they were, near the end of the day, the two boys and Santa. We expected them to kick the dog and have the women the scatter. Would this end like the shootout at the O.K corral at high noon? These boys were fully intent on disproving my very existence right then and there. Knowing them both was going to make this encounter fun. This was going to be an interesting showdown. After several "you go first…no you go…no you go…" jousting moments, Parker moved nearest me. His litmus tests were the beard had to be real and I had to know his name. Inviting him to pull the beard, my response was, "Parker, that's my beard." (Thanks to Chevy with the new "Nick" character commercials.) He said, "Well I think you are wearing a wig." I moved him past that comment by saying that as I was getting older I was losing some of my real hair and I had to wear a wig like his grandmother. She doesn't think anyone knows about her wig, but Parker does. He was satisfied. Magic!

Then it was Drew's turn. He had three tests for Santa: knowing his name, his mother's name and if he had any brothers or sisters. His name was easy. Since I knew he was an only child who had been adopted by his parents, that test was also easy. Then I said to his mother while he was next to me, "Mary, Drew here wants me to verify he has no other brothers or sisters. Knowing he doesn't is the easy part, but he wants you to say so as well." He was satisfied, at least for one more year. But, the magic was there. You never know if indeed it would be. Performance mode helps create the magic, and it appears again and again. HO HO HO, HO HO HO, HO HO HO!!!

Since this was a Downtown Christmas Experience Committee fundraising project, at ARTWORKS, several shop keepers came into the store to see what was happening and to see Santa. Word was spreading. One shop owner heard the "HO HO HO, HO HO HO, HO HO HO!!!" coming from my mouth and she wanted to know if Santa would be available for her shop in a couple of weeks. It took about one second to say yes. After all, appearing too eager might not look good. You can bet the Claus will be in the store!!!

At the suggestion of my bride, the purchase of my own Santa Suit became a priority. WOOHOO!!! A week later it came by the brown truck. It had been made for someone of my uh-umm size. But the belt was huge, really huge, two of me huge. A little alteration from my leather-smith friend and voila! "The Claus" is born.

THE MOST UNLIKELY PLACE

The Activities Director at the nursing home where my Sister-in-Law was been a resident for over ten years learned that I had dabbled at being "The Claus". She asked if Santa could make an appearance on "The Festival of Lights Night", one of the nights of the year when the nursing home has another open house. Residents that are able are given a chance to "party" with the other residents, staff and guests.

The plans for the night seemed to be the beginning one of many appearances where Santa was able to make them up as he went. The broad plan was to be "The Claus" for the children, then visit the residents. Wait a minute, children? What children? Isn't Santa going to a nursing home? This was going to be a unique experience. I wanted to verify that Santa was allowed to say "Merry Christmas." The Activities Director told me I'd better.

Finally arriving by Jeep Sleigh, the pre-arranged secret signal to begin was given. A minute later Santa burst through the door and shouted "Merry Christmas" to all. Residents, family and staff were all scattered throughout the facility. Knowing a few people allowed me to move about and greet them easily. Calling them by name helped create the Magic! Many were surprised because they couldn't figure out who I really was.

It was time to be "The Claus" for the children. A plastic decoration made to look like a Victorian fireplace scene was hung on an office wall. The open house was for the staff as well and each brought their children to do the Santa thing. The Santa chair was set in place to meet the children. "HO HO HO!!!". Most were under three and terrified of me. Once they received a candy cane their terror began to melt like the candy cane they began to eat. The staff took photos and Santa ate cookies. "HO HO HO!!!" Lots of Cookies! "HO HO HO!!!"

After visiting with the children we settled in for the real reason of the gig, visiting with the residents. Santa made a visit to every room of the nursing home. 140 people normally call this place home. There are people that have the use of their bodies but not their minds and people that have the use of their minds but not their bodies. There are people who need assistance eating and people who need assistance breathing. There are people who can be mobile with the use of a wheel chair and people who are bedridden. Fourteen people were out for the evening and, of those remaining, 100 were awake. Only four residents auditioned for the part of Ebenezer. "Bah Humbug."

Somewhere along the way a Frosty the Snowman lookalike joined in the activities. Fearing for the very life of Frosty, (the place was warm, and she was melting), we moved quickly through the halls and into the rooms. The magic was electrifying. The magic came as every resident to a person smiled or waved or just said Merry Christmas back to me—except of course the four Scrooge stand-ins. The magic was intensified when we entered the Great dining hall, Residents had been gathered for the evening's entertainment: the Karaoke singer. Speaking to each person by name created quite a buzz among the residents. The excitement was building. This was a feat that most residents, guests and staff seemed to be impressed with. After finishing the gig as "The Claus," several staff members used the words "the best ever" again. I wish they wouldn't. I can't be the best ever. I am just trying to fit in to being "The Claus"

SPECIAL NEEDED MAGIC

Having been asked to be the Claus for special needs children in the city where I call home sounded like a real challenge. Without any previous experience to go by preparation was a venture into unfamiliar territory. Each Santa opportunity is unique and has its own dynamics. And surely this event would not be any different.

Being the Claus for children in various stages of mental development was certainly a challenge. The Rotary Club made a very generous contribution of $200 to buy personalized gifts for these children. Santa provided special gifts for each child based on information provided by their teachers and aides. One wheelchair bound girl that loves Yorkshire terriers and horses received a Yorkshire playmate of the month calendar. A boy that lost his older brother three months ago received a locking safe to keep his memories. A girl that loves to walk around town received a pair of ear phones. A boy who loves John Deere got a new John Deere baseball cap.

But, the magic happened upon walking in the door. Prior to my coming there that day Santa had left Reindeer headbands with the names of each of Santa's traveling buddies printed on the front. There was Dasher and Dancer, Prancer and Vixen, Comet and Cupid, and Donner and Blitzen. Also Santa had provided foam red clown noses to each child. There might be a Rudolph replacement picked that day. In addition to the headbands, each child was wearing their red foam nose while we jingled the bells and walked through the building to the room where they were gathered. The magic, the WOW factor was once again right there in that room. This time the magic was in the form of ear to ear smiles each potential Rudolph had on their faces.

Children who couldn't speak, spoke with their eyes and their face filling smiles. Children that couldn't laugh, laughed with their eyes. Their eyes, how they twinkled. Their dimples, how merry. My little round belly shook when they laughed like a bowl full of jelly. "HO HO HO!!!"

For the past 35 years my Rotary Club, has provided a Christmas party complete with Santa for the children with multiple disabilities at one of the "Intermediate Unit" schools, this year was no exception. The club provided the money for gifts which the teachers and aides purchased based on each child's needs. These children were several developmental steps below what we experienced before. They are there because they don't seem to fit in with mainstreaming efforts for all children. I watched as another Santa dressed in a separate room. While some Christmas music was playing he made his entrance to the waiting children. They cheered and shouted and whistled and called him by name. One by one, each by their turn received their gifts from Santa. He was really good, maybe even the best. When he left my heart strings were tugged and I held the tears back. As I looked at the children, all I could say was "But for the grace of God, go I".

If Magic is determined by the size and duration of the smiles of children of all ages, we hit the pinnacle of MAGIC this day. It was right up there with the Siegfried and Roy making the elephant disappear. This is the WOW Factor. OH MY! I cried at the magic he was able to create.

THE GIGS 1.0

For the day, the big guy will be the Santa for a retailer here in town. I have had some retail experience and know that the number one way to have people to spend money in a store is to get them inside the store. The shopkeeper did her part by advertising in advance that Santa would be there. Well that alone would bring the customers into the store… in droves… or not. But there was a part for me to play as well. If there were times when I wasn't busy with a child filled lap, then something else should be done to look busy. Going outside to wave at passers-by was an option. This effort seemed to show the shop keeper that Santa was "earning" his pay. It also got me out into the cold when the times my new suit was too warm.

The chair, the throne for the Claus, was used for several visiting impressionable children with their own perception of what Santa should be or is. Jasmine, a young lady on the cusp, entered the store with her sister. They walked to the chair and Jasmine pronounced to her sister Justine that he won't be coming to our house if he doesn't know your name. Immediately I let Justine know that "Jasmine was right, because if I didn't know your name Justine, the reindeer and Santa wouldn't be able to find your house." Jasmine all the sudden was on my side of the cusp. Just a little magic. "HO HO HO, HO HO HO, HO HO HO!!!"

But the real magic that day came in the eyes and facial expressions of an eighteen month old boy. As a stranger to him I was dressed differently than anyone else he had decided it was okay to be passed to. He sat on my lap for several minutes, alternately looking deep into my eyes and looking away. Each time he looked, his apprehensions faded. He would look deeply at me, we would smile together. Without saying a word. He would touch my beard and smile. He became animated and laughed almost as if were tickling him. And I laughed when I saw him in spite of myself.

"HO HO HO, HO HO HO, HO HO HO," "HO HO HO, HO HO HO, HO HO HO!!!" It is interesting when that is done out loud. Children of all ages smile first then usually laugh. It is an expression that comes from down deep in my diaphragm and people can't help but respond. Magic! "HO HO HO!!!" It was said that they had never seen such an animated vocal Santa and once again the words "you are the best we have ever seen" are uttered. When someone tells you that, "you are the best they have ever seen", you have to wonder if they either have lived a very sheltered life, or you are truly the best, or the truth is somewhere in between. The difficult part is to know when to believe your own press.

CHUCK AND SUSAN'S HOME

My first home party as "The Claus," offered new opportunities. Here Santa visits a house full of people and gets away with stuff he couldn't do otherwise: Jingle the sleigh bells, Burst through the door, shout "Merry Christmas!" (No ACLU here), give out some gifts, and interact with the people. "HO HO HO!!!"

When we were all seated (Santa had the place of honor in the rocker) the adults on the couches etc. and the children were nestled snug on the floor, I saw him, a lad of about 11 or 12. He would be my foil. If Santa could get him on his side perhaps some of other 15 younger children might be there as well. I opened my Santa's Top Secret Naughty or Nice List and asked him his name. He said "Luke". Looking back to the list and back to him, moaned and verified the spelling of his name L-U-K-E, looking back to my list and looking up again said "You still have a couple of days to turn this around." He laughed and so did all the other children. He blushed when asked "if he had gotten caught, or was it just our secret." The magic came when all the children laughed.

When all the children received their presents from my red bag they opened them faster than down flew from a thistle. I thought I was to be there 15-20 minutes or so and was already up to ½ hour. With no real plan in place I was moving to leave and I was stopped by the father who asked me to read my poem. Sure, I'll read it. Or recite it would be a better way to describe what I did. The adults seem to be amazed that I had the Reindeer's names, all in the correct order. And that my belly shook like a bowl full of jelly brought laughter from all. "HO HO HO, HO HO HO, HO HO HO!!!" Too soon it was "Happy Christmas to all, and to all a Good Night." Once again it was said about being the best. The comparison seemed to be based on last year's Santa who was quiet and didn't interact at all.

KEEPING IT FROM THE NEIGHBORS, OR NOT

Despite my very best efforts to hide my identity as Santa from the neighborhood children, I was not entirely successful. Our next door neighbor's daughter saw me leaving for a Santa gig dressed as "The Claus." She must have told her mother, because her mother asked if she could gather her four daughters and her five grandchildren under age four together, would Santa possibly consider coming to her house as "The Claus". She said she wanted them all to have the best visit ever by Santa. There is that word again... best.

On the agreed upon date and time Santa stood outside a window and jingled the sleigh bells. Soon all five children were looking out the window with wondering eyes at what appeared. No miniature sleigh or eight tiny reindeer but a not so little driver so lively and quick. Santa pushed through the front door and shouted "Merry Christmas everybody" Oh my! What squeals of delight that "The Claus" should visit Grandma's house. The excitement and energy in the room could have lit up half the city for hours. The oldest boy must have had springs on his feet for he jumped and jumped and jumped some more for joy. And then he jumped some more. Magic! Santa gave each child a gift and a candy cane and then recited 'Twas the Night Before Christmas'. Months later the children still remembered when Santa came to Grandma's house, where not a creature was stirring not even a mouse.

Here were five children, all under age four, all very excited, and all not unbelieving that Santa would come to see them. The high-energy excitement created by the sudden appearance of Santa was something to behold, something that only children can provide. Their enthusiasm was very magical. Before he left all the children gave "The Claus" a big hug.

THE FRUITS OF MY LABORS

When the folks from the Downtown Christmas Committee had asked me to be "The Claus" this year, it was unclear anything else would come of the appearance. It did. One of the elves from that day very timidly asked if "The Claus" could make an appearance on Christmas Eve. Responding that Santa usually went to church on Christmas Eve, but beyond that, he could be available. Nothing more was said. Then about 2 weeks later we connected again and she asked me to make an appearance on Christmas Eve. She replied, "She didn't want to take away from any family time, and she understood, but was it at all possible that Santa could be at her house for no more than 15 minutes and that they would more than compensate me for my time." Compensate me for my time… ummm! Interesting!

After altering my schedule a bit by agreeing to be the minister at the nursing home and do a Christmas Eve service at 2:30PM. Santa was able be at church with his bride of 23 years and get home in time to have Christmas Eve dinner with visiting family. Santa was now free for a Christmas Eve visit. I suited up, white bearded up, and had the red peddler's sack filled with the gifts they had given me in advance. Got in the Jeep sleigh and drove to the address. While ringing the jingle bells and burst in the door. There was a party going on there with about 30 people attending. Conner, age two and Natalee, age seven were to be the focus of the visit. "Pappy and Nana" were there so they were selected as the perfect foils.

Once Santa first got there, Santa had to re-check the Top Secret Naughty and Nice list. Why, it must be a misprint but there they were, big as life on the naughty list "Pappy and Nana." Laughter permeated the room. Magic! Like a straight man waiting for a joke to happen, Nana says she had been pretty naughty sometimes in her life. More Laughter. Magic! All the nervous tension was dispelled.

It continued when asked if she was sure she wanted to talk about it in front of all these people. More real laughter. From the heart laughter… laughter given with love. Magic! Conner was as excited as I had come to expect from a child his age but Natalee was going to be the biggest challenge of the season.

The warning had been given that she had figured which family member was wearing the traveling family Santa suit for each of the last three years. We had been extra careful to be sure my beard was completely covered. She had never met me and part of my picking on "Pappy" was so she would be sure that he was in the room and visible. Santa gave out the gifts from the red peddlers sack… and recited his favorite poem to the delight of all.

The Magic was like a slow burn. It was like eating HOT chili that you think isn't hot because it doesn't start out hot. It builds up until your taste buds scream out, WOW! THAT'S HOT! Before starting with the poem we positioned Conner on my right knee and Natalee on my left. As I was naming the reindeer Natalee asked how I knew their names. I told her the story was about me and they were my reindeer. Slow burning, magic. She spent the rest of the poem studying my face, my beard, my teeth, my hat, my beard, my white fur collar, my beard. Slow burning, magic. She especially looked at my beard when we got to the part in the poem that says "his beard was white as snow" Slow burning Magic. Upon finishing Natalee was satisfied that the person whose lap she was sitting on, wasn't someone she knew or wearing the same suit she had seen before. For a moment in time enough Magic was created for her to believe.

The Magic is reflected in the eyes. There is a fine line between: boy, this is great, and when the eyes start to twinkle and the face lights up. The Magic becomes apparent when the smile starts and then fills the whole face. The Magic is really great to capture and enjoy. It usually happens once but when it does it can't be mistaken for any other emotion. Magic is why I will be The Claus next year. So much to do, to prepare…

NON-NECESSARY
NON-ESSENTIAL STUFF*

*Self-promotional stuff

Using what I have learned about marketing and promotion, it is necessary to set a plan in place to get my name out in front of the potential believers in Magic. It is also important to create a sense of urgency, so people would make sincere requests for a visit from the Claus sooner. Repeat customers are the most satisfied and the most likely to tell someone else. So, I offered repeat clients a visit with the Claus first. Dates really started to fill rapidly.

I was able to start allowing the magic to grow with others. By letting the design department at the North Pole create a cleverly worded brochure with some photos of the Claus with children. My plan is to give to all business owners in the city a brochure. The incentive is "dates are filling rapidly" (a small stretch) but demand is created when people think something isn't or won't be available. Magic! I'm old enough to remember when Johnny Carson said that there was a shortage of T paper and the next day and lasting for six months, there was a nationwide shortage of T paper. People were beaten up for taking the last roll.

The brochures are very nice looking and 500 looked like a large box full of brochures, but they started to run out quickly. To increase my efforts, the same department create business cards. I have the utmost confidence in the design department and they didn't disappoint me.

"Nick the Claus" is now printed on a beautiful card and 1,000 will last a much longer time than the brochure. They also seemed to create the same urgency. Magic!

NECESSARY,
ESSENTIAL STUFF*

*Compliance with Government regulations
or PAYING THE MAN

My efforts at self-promotion as the Claus, took me to several businesses here in town, including all the day care facilities and the intermediate units. One day care administrator asked If Santa had the fingerprint check and the necessary background checks to volunteer to work with children. OOOOOPS!

I hitched a ride on the information super highway and found out what was necessary. Paid the $37.50 and had my fingerprints applied to a document electronically. I needed two money orders of $10 (they don't take checks) for the state background checks as well. I needed a criminal history background and child abuse history check. Each is $10 but you can't get the child abuse history until you have the criminal history check and the fingerprint check. And you can't have the criminal history until you have the fingerprint check... And so it goes.

Because I have a business here in town I am on friendly speaking terms with the postal clerks at our post office. As soon as I asked for two $10 money orders, the clerk asked me if Santa was getting a background check. Magic!

I was notified by the FAA that the nine of us had to take a continuing education class on propulsion and air traffic control. I sent them a reply stating that we had delivered presents to 822.6 houses per second last year (tying the record set in 2004) and if five seconds passed before ATC identified me, we will have moved over 5,000 locations. Travelling at an incredible 650 miles per second in the 31 hours available (due to time zone changes and rotation of the earth) Santa will have visited 91.8 million homes. By the time you read this paragraph we could have been to 160,000 different houses. Magic! I passed! Well, well, I am now legal. WOOHOO!!! "HO HO HO!!!"

HAVING A LIFE OF ITS OWN

Since a lot of people knew that I was the Claus, they were more than willing to convey both the negative and positive experiences their children or grandchildren had with a Claus. If I heard it once I heard it 143 times that the first thing children "feel" about a Claus is that he isn't the real Santa. The number one reason that children give, is if they can sense that the beard is not real. If it isn't real then that guy must not be real either. This is especially true in the three to seven year age group.

By Christmas I had 8-9 months of growth and was well into the third jar of the magic whitener. It was also true that it couldn't be pulled from my chin. It is real.

Ok, it grew for the season and it was colored white for the gigs. Some people said they liked it; other people said they didn't. I knew I wasn't Bret Keisel, but I realized I could emulate what he does on the local level. He shaves off his beard for charity after the Steelers complete their season. Those that liked my beard had a chance to vote by paying a dollar. Those that didn't like my beard also had a chance to vote by paying a dollar. It didn't matter what their opinions were; simple democracy would decide the outcome. Whichever side generated the most dollars–uh votes–would win. Simple democracy. All the money would go to my favorite charity– The Rotary Foundation, for the World Wide Eradication of Polio. I expected to raise about $50.00 and after Christmas I would either shave it off or keep it. Soon, the plan morphed into something bigger and far different.

At a meeting and I had just told people how they could also vote. Someone offered up the idea of a third option. Shave my head and keep the beard. The wheels turned and it was decided it could be something bigger so I was willing to run with it. Shave the beard… keep the beard… shave my head.

Having no expectations as to how much money this would raise it would be interesting to tally the results. I was in charge of our annual pancake breakfast and the fundraising was for Rotary's Polio eradication, it could be shaved at the breakfast. The next part was to find someone willing to do the shaving. When the District Governor heard about my plans, she said she wanted to be the one to do the shaving. OH MY!

My part was to promote the vote and soon it was very clear Santa would be bald and still have a beard when the fun was over. From November 1st until the following March 31st, I had collected $1,800 dollars' worth of votes which would pay for 3,000 doses of Polio vaccine. For a short period of time Santa had a full beard and shaved head. It was Magic!

SUMMER DOWN TIME

Previously the city hosted an "Anything That Floats" race on the river. For some reason the inspiration popped into my head to create a craft using 2 liter soda pop bottles for flotation. I had nothing beyond that... just an idea. Most people would laugh at such a crazy idea. But they laughed at Noah and Columbus as well. With no plan in mind, my wife and I started to collect empty 2 liter soda pop bottles. As their number grew so did her dismay. Her perception was, that there were too many bottles everywhere. Several times we discussed the issue of the growing number of bottles. Well, she discussed and I listened. We only had collected 50 or so, but, they were getting in the way. What was I going to do with them anyway? I smiled knowing some vague idea was still floating around in my head.

What's the plan? Indiana Jones once replied when asked that question, "I don't know... I am making it up as I go." Make a raft by placing a piece of plywood on top of the empty bottles? Sides would necessary so it would not swamp. So how about a sleigh? A bright Red Santa Sleigh/boat... out of place (on the river)... dream on, Columbus. I do not have the tools or the skill to craft a sleigh. Besides it can be said that I have enough knowledge about power tools to avoid a major accident. I always remember my high school shop teacher showing the class his left hand with his three middle fingers cut off and telling us that we were to be careful with power tools or our hands would look like his. A sleigh? In the water? I must be crazy!

In May I visited Denny and Sue, clients of mine living 90 miles away. Once we completed the business, the small talk turned to my vague sleigh/boat plan. It turns out that while I was lamenting about not having the proper tools to make the sleigh he was thinking of his basement woodworking shop. He actually showed me one of the miniature sleighs he had made with his scroll saw. It was very nice but a water bottle would be all it needed to keep it afloat. His work was about 1/10th of the size that I wanted so I really had no hope that anything could develop from the conversation.

Sometimes you are good and sometimes you are lucky. I was not good by any stretch, but luck played a big part. On a Saturday afternoon four days later we had a driving late spring rain. My soaking wet client, Denny knocked at my door. He told me to get out there before we both got more soaked and help get this sleigh out of his truck. There it was a life size sleigh that he had made. I was overwhelmed. Now I had to follow through and actually do something with it. This year the city was planning an "Anything That Floats" race as part of the River Fest on August 18th. So now I had a sleigh, and 65 bottles. Now was the time to make it work. There would be no elf design team, just me. Dream and talk; or dream and do.

When the caulking was finished the sleigh/boat was painted a very bright red and white by using marine paint. It looked great. It was as if the design team at the North-pole had really done the work. Now came the bottles. It didn't take too long for me to realize that it was going to take a lot more than the 65 we had collected to complete the project. Since time was running out I asked all my friends and neighbors to save 2 liter bottles for the project. You would think that it was the most complex engineering feat ever accomplished as almost everyone wanted to know how it was done. The temptation was to say the elves did it by magic but a quick visual check and anyone could see the screws. The installation was deceptively simple. I marked the location of each bottle. One at a time, I unscrewed the caps, used my cordless screwdriver and ½ inch wood screws to attach the caps to the bottom of the craft, and then I tightened the bottles onto the fixed caps.

On Monday August 13, the last bottle was collected and installed. Eleven rows of eleven and ten rows of ten. 221 bottles in all were screwed on the sleigh. The hardest part had been collecting the bottles. Now all the bottles are in place on the sleigh/boat. Now, for the next challenge, I had to find a pool to test the contraption.

My neighbor Joe, owns an in-ground pool. As the project progressed I had asked him if it would be possible to see if it floated. He said several times that when it is finished, he would decide. Watching the last bottle being applied to the craft, He finally said, He would allow me to see if it would float that evening. He had never let anyone outside the family in his pool since he had it built in 1987. I was honored. Not only had that... he said his three adult sons would help me put it in the water. WOW! Two of them did not think it would float.

Now, the problem was to work out the logistics and eat dinner as well. The sleigh with the 221 bottles attached to the bottom would not clear the gate in his fence. All the bottles had to be removed, before his three sons finished eating and got to my garage door in 45 minutes. To complicate things my bride had dinner ready and it was getting cold. I had all the bottles off and then they carried the bright red sleigh/boat through the gate and to the pool. Once inside the gate we reattached all the bottles in much the same way they came off. Once that chore was complete we turned it "right side to" and moved it into the pool.

Being the only one with a bathing suit was reason enough to have me in the water as we guided it into the pool. OH MY! IT WORKED! It displaced just a tiny bit of water. It was floating in the pool. Now, the real test. The big guy had to get in. Knowing that violating the rule of gravity was a possibility, it was necessary to place my rather large frame in the middle of the sleigh/boat. I climbed on board. IT WORKED! It went about two inches deeper into the water. WOOHOO! The sleigh and the big guy were on the water and we weren't sinking. WOOHOO! Got the kayak oars and maneuvered in the pool. I was so happy. "HO HO HO!!!" Magic!

Now for the real test, putting the sleigh in the river. The "Anything That Floats" race was cancelled at the last minute. My guess is they were overwhelmed by my sleigh/boat competition. But, I still wanted to put the sleigh in the water. I needed to know that my idea would actually work and that the final follow through was necessary. I also need to know for Denny, the great person that made it and delivered it to me on a rainy afternoon. He had made such an effort and he could not be let down. It floated in a pool. It was maneuverable in a pool. What would it do in the current of the Yough River?

The day arrived and two men from the neighborhood agreed to help me put the sleigh/boat in the water. On August 18th at 1:30PM we loaded the sleigh onto my pickup and all the empty bottles in big plastic bags and we were off. Within three minutes we were reapplying the 2 liter bottles. I had an assortment of "Coke" bottles and "Pepsi" bottles (There is a difference in the bottles both in size and shape.) as well an assortment of green and clear bottles. There were enough green bottles to surround the perimeter. The "Coke" bottles are about ¾ of an inch higher than the "Pepsi" bottles. There were 48 Coke and 173 Pepsi bottles. One could probably do a marketing sample of the neighborhood and state that Pepsi was more popular by a four to one margin, but I digress.

Grouping the coke bottles together in two sets of two rows and putting a coke bottle on each corner and in the middle of each end gave it the even weight distribution that would not crush the bottles when we turned the sleigh "right side to". This is such a marvelous highly technical phrase. Red duct tape would hold the bottles in place and prevent a disaster if the sleigh/boat ran upon a shallow spot and the rocks caught the bottom. Bottles in place, tape in place, sleigh turned right side to… Now, to be the Claus; Red Tee shirt, Red life vest, Red kayak oars, Red Santa Hat, Sunglasses, and Whitened beard. Nick was ready.

Several people had gathered and they began to take pictures. Some people suggested that it would never float. I was asked, "If I had tested it" or "if I had taken complete leave of my senses". As I heard their comments I kept thinking that were earning a place on the naughty list.

Put it in the water and float or sink. With the gathered crowd watching and taking pictures, floating would be better. We put it in the water or should I say on the water. There was so much buoyancy that it displaced very little water and when I got in, it was like floating on air. It was a very good thing as the river water level was very low due to the recent drought. I paddled out about 30 yards floated with the current turned around paddled against the current and had a great but short-lived time. It was Magic and many people took pictures to capture the moment. My only problem was that my kayak oars were about a foot too short.

My vague plan worked and a full year of effort and planning was a huge success. It is such a great feeling! I know the elves will make this day, the topic of discussion.

NEW SEASON, COMPLETE WITH NEW FRUSTRATIONS

THE CLAUS 3.0

Like the baseball player that closed out last season with a game winning grand slam in the World Series, (you're the best ever) it is time to check the uniform and stretch the legs. The new season starts and the show must go on. In baseball you are only as good as your last hit. In sales it has been said that you are only as good as your next sale. I'm only as good as the next believer in magic. It is time for a reality check here. I'm not the best Santa ever, therefore, I have to work harder to create magic.

On August 31st of the year, (opening day of training camp) I received a call from the Christmas Shop in a small town in the mountains. The brochures are beginning to pay off. For several years they have had an event in the fall that focused on fall stuff... foliage and fall leaf color changes to be exact. They threw in vendors who display and sell their crafts and wares. In years past they attracted as many as two to three thousand people. The plan was to be there from 11:00 in the morning till 3:00 in the afternoon on a Saturday at the end of September. Sit on the throne and be Santa for the children.

It was easy to know how a head coach feels when confronted with an injury to a starting player in the middle of training camp, just ten days before the event, the need to replace the Elf became apparent. The bottom line is just as a magician needs an assistant to make illusions work, I needed an Elf. An Elf is needed to do the Elf magic before the children sit on Santa's lap. Spending days asking everyone I knew, if they knew someone that might be willing to work as an Elf and be willing to split whatever we made in tips. Although everyone was empathetic, we were unable to locate an Elf. Calling the head Elf at the North Pole would not work. This was the week the toy factory shut down for retooling for some of the new toys. It also allows everyone to catch their collective breath take a vacation and gear up for Christmas Eve.

As luck would have it, while at the grocery store on Monday, I bumped into the teacher from the High School that was in charge of the musicals. He surely would know someone. It seemed that a warm body would do but if anyone was available he would know about them. He said he had someone in mind and would let me know. As these things go, the neighborhood girl agreed to be an Elf right then and there. Later the phone rang it was from that teacher and he said he had located someone. I had to tell him that I had found someone else in my desperation. I was very clear to thank him for his efforts. To say he was upset would be to put it mildly. He indicated if he had known I was going to ask someone else he would not have put any effort into my request. After all, he said he had spent all evening working on my request.

For a while the guilt worked on me thinking he was right. He had that special knack for making me feel as guilty as my mother had been so good at doing so many years ago. As these things go, I really couldn't call him anyway as I had given him, my information but he did not give me his. He brings out the best in all the kids and was only holding me to the same standard.

On Tuesday the neighbor girl that had volunteered on Monday came to me as soon as my day was finished. She was very sorry but she had been unaware of a softball commitment her coach had made for the upcoming Saturday. Her team would be playing 6 games. The Santa gig was now doomed to run without an Elf. It would be do-able but difficult.

While anticipating the taste of undesired crow, another call was made to the teacher. After a healthy dose of crow feeding he said he would make a call and see if he could help me out. He reminded me how disappointed the girls were that I had asked someone else. I got it! I just need an Elf. (He never suspected that my crow had turned me bitter.)

The sale begins once someone says no. The next step was to ask, with a smile in my voice and crow in my belly, if he could help me out. MAGIC! He mellowed and said he would make a call or two and get back with me, BUT, he did not want me to call anyone else until he called. We agreed with my politest "Yes sir". Seven minutes later, he returned the call with the names of two girls, the mother of one wanted me to call her and explain what I needed. She would make the decision for both girls. As soon as the phone was answered I was ready to explain how disappointed the children would be without the very important Elf at Santa's side. The drama teacher wasn't the only one who could lay the guilt on… As it turned out, I really didn't have to say anything, because she had already decided it would be a great experience.

She told me that both girls would meet me in the parking lot of the major grocery store in town at 9:30AM SHARP! 9:30AM came and went. Santa was getting very nervous. 9:31… 9:32… 9:33…9:34… Suddenly the proverb came to me stating that a man that has two watches never knows what time it is, but, a man that has one watch always knows what time it is. I called my bride to ask her to search my scribbled notes to locate and provide me with the mother's number to see if I had misunderstood the plan was the next logical course of action. Just as my bride found the paper with my scribbled notes, (I probably should have been a doctor) a Yellow VW bug drove up. Since it was a newer VW with the engine in the front, somehow, it struck me that my Elves had arrived. My deduction was correct.

Not only were they there but Sarah's mother had crafted Elf clothing for both Sarah and Marina. She is so gifted and they really looked like the honor guard Elves at the North Pole. They were from the drama department their creativity would help them move into the roles they needed to play.

At the end of the season last year my leather-smith friend was contacted to provide him with some more business. One of the things he does well is crafting sleigh bells using real leather for the strap. He would not use a plastic strap with riveted cheap bells that were so readily available from the box stores. He said he would make one for me and asked if Santa wanted four, five or six bells. Six bells of course, has a nice ring to it doesn't it? When he gave me the price he was paid. Then the waiting began. And we waited and waited and waited. Nine months later and just a mere ten days before my event it was necessary to call him again. This is when he informed me that he had the large size and the small size bells but he had just this week received the two mid-sized bells he needed. He put it on the big brown truck and they arrived with four days to spare. This is a classic example of the adage, "If it weren't for the last minute… nothing would get done."

My bride always wants me to look my best when leaving home. Whether it was for work, or for Rotary, or when I am a lay minister, she sees to it that I look my best. This is a role she has taken upon herself since we first met. This time was no exception the task has not always been easy. She had been the one to see to it that the suit that fit was ordered.

Also, to her credit, she succeeded in convincing me that throwing away two pair of shoes this year was best. Having retrieved them from the garbage can, yes garbage can, twice and thinking about keeping them and getting them repaired didn't seem to garner any favor with my bride. My shoes were with me through thick and thin. We had walked together for more than a mile and they were hard to part with. The problem was now the thin was thinner than it should have been. Paul Harvey once quoted a study that determined the key to a successful and long lasting marriage. After much build up, he simply said that success in a marriage, depended on the man's ability to say "Yes, Dear." So maybe she does know best. It would probably be best if she didn't know I conceded that fact.

It wasn't really a surprise when she asked about my hair. She thought a white wig was in order. It became a point of contention only because she did not know about the direction I was planning to take. Since the event was before Halloween (Yes, it is always Christmas at the Christmas Shop) it would be easy to get some spray-on white stuff and not have to wear a wig. We stopped at two stores on a trip home from the big city and sure enough, at the second one, there it was in aisle 15, spray-on white stuff. My hair would be white, with no wig, WOOHOO! Eventually wearing a wig was indeed better. "Yes Dear."

Since it was still September and we hadn't yet unpacked my black boots as they had been packed away with the winter clothes. Well, part of the costume includes black fake boot covers that give the illusion of wearing full boots. It took me several minutes to convince her that I could wear black shoes and get the same effect.

The next item was the "naughty or nice" list. The paper list from last year was tearing and looking as if it should have thrown it away. The wear and tear gave it some character. But, once again wisdom ruled over convenience and another opportunity to say, "Yes, dear" popped up. My bride asked our crafty daughter in law for help and the two of them crafted a permanent made of cloth N & N list complete with invisible ink. In my best Santa voice came my approval. "Yes Dear."

The morning of the event we were hitting on all cylinders. The Claus was suited up, had a white beard and hair when the daughter in law suggested rosy cheeks. What? They are rosy aren't they? Apparently they weren't. That issue was solved with the application of something from a tube or jar or... whatever it was she had. "Yes Dear."

As the belt was placed around my waist I realized that last year my girth had stretched the holes in the belt beyond normal use parameters a bit and the grommets were broken. A new belt would soon be in order. Well I do have a leather smith friend... "HO HO HO, HO HO HO, HO HO HO!!!" The new season has kicked off and I can't wait to help children believe in the magic.

THE GIGS 2.0

With the Elves as my passengers, my hair and beard whitened my cheeks rosy and the red suit under plastic, and the N & N list created, we were off in the pick-up sleigh. As we travelled the 35 miles it became necessary to tell the Elves about their job being the most important job in the search for Magic and without their handling their job properly, Magic, is elusive and extremely difficult to find. They had been recommended as two of the brightest and best so they would live up to the billing. Almost instantly, they seemed to have a full understanding of what was expected.

Asking them if they had thought about Elf names brought the negative response. Two teen-aged girls, smart-phones with instant Google access provided names that couldn't be wished on a dog. Urging them to put their creative heads together and come up with more Elf-like names. After about 3 seconds they in unison said "Sarah and Marina". Not much of a reach here, but they explained "Sarah" was classic enough to be believable and "Marina" was just whimsical enough. Gee, why didn't Santa think of that?

We arrived and got the lay of the land. We checked out the restroom facilities (always a very important thing to know) and where the Santa Throne was. I let Sarah and Marina wander around. I believe it was colder then we all thought it might be and they were getting cold already. Santa was dressed in fur from his head to his foot and not cold.

Unable to locate a phone booth like superman, it was necessary to use the restroom to become Santa. Red fur pants and coat, boots, belt, hat, gloves and I was ready. In short order, I morphed into the Claus. We spent a few minutes walking through the grounds to meet all the vendors and get a feel for what they are selling. Then it was time to sit on the throne, this was a real leather wing back throne, not the old porcelain kind. It wasn't long before the first child of the day sought my attention. He is in 5th grade and definitely on the cusp. I could tell by his questions he was checking out my validity. He wanted to know what my favorite Santa movie was… The Santa Clause. Then I asked him what his favorite Santa movie was, he replied The Polar Express. We agreed "What a great movie". Then the task was to bring him back from the edge of disbelief, I echoed the idea that as long as you could hear the bell, Santa was real. Without any prompting, but precisely on cue the photographer rang a sleigh bell, I'm sure it produced a sound that many people couldn't hear but since his eyes twinkled I knew he did. Magic!

One girl who looked to be about 3 asked her mother, why there were two Santas? Another young girl came with her sister and little brother Warren. Warren was terribly unsure about the whole thing and the pooched lips and tears welled up immediately. But, Cloe knew what she wanted and a team of wild reindeer couldn't keep her back.

This 2 year old leaving the comfort of her father's arms knew that she had nothing to fear, ran to be with Santa. Her family could hardly keep up. I received a hug that was as strong as a 2 year old could manage and she wasn't about to let go of my neck. Magic! Perhaps it was because the veins in my neck began to bulge and my face was like a cherry. She was holding tight, so tight that the parents thought they might have to step in and release me. I had to wave them back and the Magic kept growing. Carrying her to the big chair with her hugging me and her smile was as beautiful as they get. "This, is why I do this"… I thought to myself. She and her siblings created Magic just by being there. But her hug and beautiful smile prompted me to forget the minor frustrations before this day. "HO HO HO!!!"

Throughout the day several children found their way to the throne and all were amazed that Santa knew their names. The Elves were doing a great job. Each child told me they were good and they always listened to and did what their parents said. I believe that some had their fingers crossed as they talked. I told each of them that it was very important to continue being good, listen to their parents and I would visit them on Christmas Eve. Santa also let it be known that he liked cookies and milk and that Vixen just absolutely loved carrots.

They had an antique rocking chair and Santa was comfortable sitting in it as it was outside. Most people were able to see me there and I was rather warm sitting on the throne (I was wearing fur from my head to my foot) even though the Elves were perpetually cold that day. A local peewee football team was at the festival trying to raise money for necessary equipment. They brought their cheerleaders with them. I think the entire group decided that none of them were going to sit on Santa's lap. I could sense the disappointment from some of the children...

As the day progressed, it was apparent that if they weren't coming to Santa so Santa would go to them. It was an easy move to go where they were and call them each by name. When each was asked a question they all suddenly turned shy, but, the conversation was productive in getting a response from each one. The peer pressure was very great not to sit on the big guy's lap.

One girl maybe six years old, natural blonde and cute as a button, named Haley found it very difficult not to run up and sit in the lap of someone who could bring her a dream or two. She would position herself just out of my line of vision (she thought) and when she thought the others weren't looking she would wave. Santa saw it out of the corner of his eye thinking at first that he really didn't see it. The wave was not a fake model wave as so many girls do today, but, a real honest to goodness from the heart wave. She moved it up and down waving from the elbow. I could see her hand move, but I knew something special was happening. I knew there was a smile attached to that wave. I'll bet she waved over 20 times. With each wave she would move just slightly more into view. She was banking on the fact that the other kids couldn't see her wave. And each of her waves got a return wave back. Then she started peeking around the corner to make sure I saw the wave. I leaned over to my side and waved and smiled back and her repeated smile was Magic. "HO HO HO, HO HO HO, HO HO HO!!!"

BFF (BEST FRIEND FOREVER)

About a month before the season got in full swing, the requests for Nick became more creative and frequent. One came from my Vet. Yes, the very same Doctor that treats my dogs, cats and other animals as well. The plan was to be available so owners could present their pets to have their photos with Santa. Pets and Santa… Sounds like a simple plan. What could possibly go wrong?

This would be a nice opportunity to get back into Santa mode without any children to provide uncomfortable situations. The time was from 10:00AM until 2:00PM. The plans were loose, other than the times they had established. They had never done anything like that before. They decided that they would offer their clientele the time slots between 9:00am and 11:00am and the general public between 11:00AM and 1:00PM. No, I'm not dumber than a box of rocks. They changed the times and failed to notify central scheduling at the North Pole. At 9:00AM the phone rang with a desperate search for the man called Nick. I told them I would be there as soon as possible and at 9:20AM, I blazed into the parking lot. I told all the waiting folks that we had had an unfortunate accident. The neighbor's Grandma got run over by one of the reindeer. There were some allegations about too much eggnog, Fortunately, Elf emergency dispatch was able to take care of Grandma's hoof marked backside. There are some things in this world that make the visual picture just hard to grasp. And this was one of them.

Nick the Claus at a vet… seems like I had come full circle and I really didn't think I would find magic. But I did… There were about 30 pets. They ranged in size from a teacup poodle at weighing in at 5 ounces, to a St. Bernard weighing in at a cool 175 pounds. The photo of Nick and Cujo's direct descendent made Nick look small by comparison. Maybe I should get a St. Bernard... ummm!!! Five cats rounded out the pet parade and photos.

Each pet was at best ok with being near me and some were very nervous about meeting a new friend. I found it interesting that none of the dogs voiced their opinion in either way. Dogs never bark when Santa is in the home. But in contemplating the day, I hit on the magic. The magic came not from the animals or the elves that help control them, but from the person attached to the other end of the leash. We have been given faithful, loving, loyal companions that don't care how our resume' reads. They provide unconditional love to enhance our lives. All they ask in return is to be fed, loved and to be a member in good standing in the pack at a location we call home.

One dog stood out in the parade of pets. It was a black long haired something mix with his life-long companion at the end of the leash. Champ was making sure his human would feel comforted by the other humans that offered him cookies and a hot cup of coffee. His human was a widower and no one knows how long Champ and he had been together. Champ wasn't sure about meeting me, but soon realized he had nothing to fear. Prior to his being the center of attention at this sea of humans all making funny noises and calling his name while making bright flashes of light. It was quite obvious that he had not left the old man's side for quite a while. After the photos were taken, the staff had the gentleman sit the "exam" room while they were printing the photo of Champ and Nick. Champ instantly became very comfortable in being near Santa. Everyone tried to coax Champ to tend to his friend but he would not leave my area. He stayed near my feet and we interacted like I had been at the other end of that leash. We became old friends at that moment... Champ and me... Magic!

I am reminded about the "story" written many years ago and widely circulated on the internet.

"An old man and his dog were walking down this dirt road with fences on both sides, they came to a gate in the fence and looked in, it was nice grassy, woody areas, just what a 'huntin' dog and man would like, but, it had a sign saying 'no trespassing' so they walked on. They came to a beautiful gate with a person in white robes standing there. "Welcome to Heaven" he said. The old man was happy and started in with his dog following him. The gatekeeper stopped him. "Dogs aren't allowed, I'm sorry but he can't come with you."

"What kind of Heaven won't allow dogs? If he can't come in, then I will stay out with him. He's been my faithful companion all his life, I can't desert him now." "Suit yourself, but I have to warn you, the Devil's on this road and he'll try to sweet talk you into his area, he'll promise you anything, but the dog can't go there either. If you won't leave the dog, you'll spend Eternity on this road."

So the old man and dog went on. They came to a rundown fence with a gap in it, no gate, just a hole. Another old man was inside. "S'cuse me Sir, my dog and I are getting mighty tired, mind if we come in and sit in the shade for awhile?" "Of course, there's some cold water under that tree over there. Make yourselves comfortable" "You're sure my dog can come in? The man down the road said dogs weren't allowed anywhere."

"Would you come in if you had to leave the dog?" "No sir, that's why I didn't go to Heaven, he said the dog couldn't come in. We'll be spending Eternity on this road, and a glass of cold water and some shade would be mighty fine right about now. But, I won't come in if my buddy here can't come too, and that's final."

The man smiled a big smile and said "Welcome to Heaven." "You mean this is Heaven? Dogs ARE allowed? How come that fellow down the road said they weren't?" "That was the Devil and he gets all the people who are willing to give up a life-long companion for a comfortable place to stay. They soon find out their mistake, but then it's too late. The dogs come here, the fickle people stay there. GOD wouldn't allow dogs to be banned from Heaven. After all, HE created them to be man's companions in life, why would he separate them in death?"

I am so very sure that cats serve in their own way as our companions and they enhance our lives. And I am so proud to include them as my friends as well. Magic!

COMMUNITY CENTER: PART 1

The first the event seemed to be disjointed. There was a set of loose plans with a lot of ideas. But, as it got closer it all began to fall in place. I had arraigned to have the sleigh/boat moved to the school and set on the stage. My bride and daughter in law created the toy bag full of toys and required that another trip be made to set it on the sleigh on stage. At the same time we completed a mike test for the activities on the second day. Upon returning home once again the Claus emerged. First came whitening of my hair, then the beard then the bright red suit for the evening. Boots and belt, glasses and hat and Claus was moving.

The New Haven Volunteer Fire Company provided my ride. Being early has always been my thing and this was no exception using the extra time to o I practice climbing up on the truck ladder and being hooking up to the safety equipment, then unhooking and climbing down. Safety was a subtle message for the children. It just would not look good if the papers had a photo of Santa on his way to the hospital having fallen off the fire truck. Besides, except when I was six years old the closest I've been to a fire truck was the required "keep back 300 feet".

Our Mayor, was the one that had to give the okay. And our devoted life saving firemen and women were in constant communication with him as the events progressed. It was an unbelievable honor to be given a ride inside the truck to a nearby parking lot. A place where very few non-official people can sit. In the lot away from the kids, Santa climbed on top of the truck to the ladder turntable. I was helped into the belt harness by the brave soul. I took my position and the belt was hooked in place. A blast from the air horn and we were ready to roll. Lights on, siren on… I'm living a dream. Mr. Mayor said bring the truck on. Oh, it was only 2 blocks that I rode on top of the truck, but I was more excited than any children might have been. We drove up the hill in front of the building that once was the old high school.

There they were. 300 people standing and shouting and waving. Santa cleared the lump in his throat and, Yelled "Merry Christmas Everybody" and then received an echo of so many voices of a "Merry Christmas Santa." Magic. It has never been better than at that moment. After being unhooked from the fireman's safety belt and not wanting the crowd to see if he stumbled. Santa climbed off the truck on the side away from the crowd. I overheard a young boy say to his father, "See dad, even Santa wears a safety belt." I'll bet the National Safety Council is jealous of that one.

Barely off the truck and the children swarmed to me. It was like a group of bees protecting the hive. Oh My! It was wonderful. Santa began to greet each and every child. Some couldn't wait to hug Santa. Often there were two children in my arms. That was perfectly okay! It was so exhilarating. For the next 2 hours the children sought out Santa. They hugged and gave hand drawn pictures and told me what they wanted. The children were all over the building and we were there to make them feel special. Oh my! Moving through the sea of humanity that contained hundreds of broad smiles from each child. Oh, the unbridled joy. They had the chance to touch Santa and be hugged by him if they dared. Oh! The hugs were so very special as each child moved from where they were to where Santa was. Because it was safe and they were with their parents, no child cried. This was probably a first in the annals of Santa visiting. The air was full of energy and I fed on that energy like I had never before. It was unscripted and it was beautiful. Magic!!!

DOWNTOWN CHRISTMAS COMMITTEE AGAIN

The Annual Downtown Christmas event once again came to the city. The third time is the charm, they say. (They are always quoted, and they seem to always be right, but I still don't know who they are.) The weather was unseasonably warm. So, more people ventured out. They came to the store seemingly by the busload. For three and a half hours Santa was permitted to enjoy the company of about 75-85 children. The store was swarmed with Children that mostly still believed. Children that wanted to sit on the big guys lap. Oh there were the usual suspects, those toddlers with great apprehension. They were the ones that would not leave the comfort of mom or dad's arms. They cried when they did not know they had nothing to fear. The two week old and even the mother due in a week all sat in my lap.

The vast majority of the children were between 4 and 7. They were filled with belief and wonder. Almost everyone in that age group had lost some of their teeth. I kept expecting each to start singing "All, I Want for Christmas Is My Two Front Teeth." One little girl in that age group was wearing what looked like new glasses. Her pout turned to a smile, when I told her how pretty she looked. I would guess her parents had been trying to persuade her to keep the glasses on and that she looked great. But she is probably like the rest of us that walk on this earth. We hear something from the people who love us that we tend not to believe, but let a stranger say the same thing and all the sudden it is like we hear and believe it for the very first time.

Towards the end of the day, a boy about 8 years old came into the room. His mother and two sisters came in as well. He did not come up to me but spoke from the door. He said, "My father died this past year, and I miss him so much." Quickly his mother pulled him back and yelled, "Joshua, Santa can't bring him back." I asked Joshua to come in and close the door and leave his mother outside. He did as I asked then he came close.

I asked if he went to church. When he said yes, I told him I was so sorry about him losing his father. I knew how he would miss him as I lost my father too. I told him when he was feeling really bad, that God would hold him in his arms and comfort him. I told him that God had a picture of him and his dad on his refrigerator. I told him that God loved him. I asked if we might pray. He said yes. I prayed that God would watch over him and his family and keep them safe today and always... I was all choked up and asked God to help me. I told him it was probably true that I couldn't bring him back. But that he had something very special. He knew his father loved him and he had special memories of the things his father did with him and no one else. I asked to remember those things and keep them in his heart.

Such mixed emotions, such a powerful moment. I was able to display my faith, even though I really felt there would be no Hallmark movie ending. OH MY! OH MY! OH MY!

My number one elf, asked if I could share what happened and when I gave the Reader's Digest condensed version, she went and talked to the mother. She is planning a Christmas present and food family adoption. God's Magic!

COMMUNITY CENTER: PART 2

It was a race. Santa had to get to the theatre before the "Polar Express" movie stopped playing. I got there as the movie was ending and got back stage and in position. Just in time. The stage was decorated with a very large tree, my bright red sleigh with a giant toy bag for all to see, and filled with bears. There was also a stool for Santa to sit on. HO HO HO!!! And "Merry Christmas" I shouted to all and they all shouted back "Merry Christmas". I hate the overworked word, "Awesome". But this was, Awesome!

Santa was center stage with a room full of parents and children. Reading the story about "Rufus the Put Away Bear" that he had written. It is based on the sleigh/boat Santa had in the garage. The bright red sleigh was going to be used as my Christmas decorations. Rufus was a renegade put away bear would steal Santa's sleigh and sell sleigh rides for a fish. He would get caught by Santa himself and he would be sorry and Santa would forgive him and give him a new put away bear mission. We had a drawing for Rufus the Put Away Bear and the cutest little girl was the lucky winner. Rufus was bigger than she was and he was very plush and soft. Later Santa was told that she actually used it to re-mop the entire floor. And that she would not let anyone take it from her. HO HO HO!!! HO HO HO!!! HO HO HO!!!

Then Santa recited the other his famous story, the one that began the whole journey. They cheered and shouted when Santa came to the line "Happy Christmas to all and to all a Good Night." Those that wanted to were able to line up and sit on Santa's lap. Being on stage is Magical enough but this experience was great. Santa was able to help children feel very good about themselves. It was also unique because we had positioned a microphone and the parents could hear what their children wanted without having to be at arm's length to do the ear strain thing. The children were less bashful without mom and dad right there. A lot of these children probably would not be making the trek to the mall so it was gratifying to be able to bring Magic to them. HO HO HO!!!

STORY TIME 1.0

The journey continued at the Carnegie Free Library here in town. A magnificent stone building that was originally donated by Andrew himself Over 100 years ago. Today, it still serves as a place where children gather to have stories read to them. One of the librarians; Judy, is enormously gifted in dealing with preschool age children. She had provided me with the name of a book I had never heard of, "The Christmas Cookie Sprinkle Snitcher". The Library did not have a copy. It became essential to make a trip to the web site of the international purveyor of every printed book ever made to see if anyone was trying to sell one of these books. Only two books were available to buy so one was going to be Santa's so the arrangements were made to have the big brown truck to deliver it. Reading two books was the plan; "The Christmas Cookie Sprinkle Snitcher" and from the hard cover copy of "The Night Before…"

It was weekly story time on a December, Wednesday morning at the library. I was Santa and they were excited… or not. They were going to be surprised and they didn't know it. That is why they call it a surprise. In the mean time they were making something special. Judy was guiding each little pair of hands to make a crafty yet very simple, 3 dimensional Santa and tree hanger complete with a name badge. Two triangles and some pre-cut face pieces to glue into place and make Santa heads. A dab of cotton and a length of yarn all put together to make a Santa ornament and name badge all in one.

I don't know what happened with the previous Santa experience, but I was told that each and every child actually hid to get out of his way. It was worse than herding a bunch of cats. I was determined not to let that happen again. I rang the sleigh bells and gave a hearty HO

HO HO!!! Merry Christmas everybody!!! They all shouted back with squeals of absolute delight. So far so good, there was no one under a chair. I moved to each child and talked to each one as they sat with mom or nana and called everyone by their name. It was a collective gasp of surprise. Actually it is just like me going to Wal-Mart and calling a cashier by her name. They always act surprised that I know their names. Magic! (It's on the name badge they are required to wear.) HO HO HO!!! Because I called each of the children by their names most of the fear went away. I made sure to complement each one on their ornament and on how nice they looked. HO HO HO!!! I am convinced that the magic is created when I know their names.

After reading the two stories with the help of the two women named Judy. They also served very well as my elves. And each child in turn came to sit on my lap. Mostly they have been told that Rudolph loves carrots. But the new piece of information for each one was that Vixen yes Vixen really loves carrots. Knowing the children's names combined with their smiles and it was a really magical time. Twelve named children, fourteen adults produced smiles all around. Santa never get tired of the smiles the magic produces. Every occasion that Santa has been available to children a Magic moment happens. This occasion was no different. The children were sitting on the floor facing the big guy with the story book. When the readings were complete a girl as blonde as blonde can be, made a special effort to move in closer and in a blink of an eye we made eye contact. Her eyes how they twinkled and her genuine smile made the day all worthwhile. Most people don't see the moments of magic, but Santa does and it is priceless.

CARNEGIE FREE LIBRARY: 3 DAYS LATER

On Saturday Santa held the top billing after the opening act from a group that very creatively acted out a story about Rudolph. It was about how Rudolf came to be, and how Santa selected him to guide the sleigh from the island of misfit toys. All the performers were under 15 and it was done very well. The director sat back stage with me and was able to "introduce" me by playing "Santa Claus Is Coming to Town". The crowd was electrified and I got them to clap in time to the music. Several children came up to see me on the big chair. Parents took pictures each was given a candy cane.

Sean couldn't make it to the program, he had been bowling and he showed up as all the other children were leaving. He looked so hopeful, he also looked left out... alone and disappointed. His mother was with him but when you are in second grade, sometimes being with mom just isn't enough. He stood in the doorway. And he was larger than life.

I immediately recognized him and I shouted out to him "Hey Sean, Merry Christmas, I was wondering if you were going to come and see me today!" His face lit up like he had just found a puppy. I am not sure if it was because I knew him or if it was because he had my undivided attention. If he had been Frosty the snowman he would have melted right then and there. The warmth was radiant and he spent several minutes talking, with me holding him on my lap. I know his mother does not have one of those newfangled telephones that take pictures as well. The memory of his visit will have to remain in his mind forever and not etched on the photo paper everyone uses. Magic. HOHOHO!!! HOHOHO!!! HOHOHO!!!

When Sean finally felt comfortable enough to leave there was a return visit for the second time by Emily. The first visit she was shy and didn't really speak. The second visit came about because she wanted to ask me a question. She wanted to know if we had received her special letter at the North Pole stating that she would be leaving that night and going to Florida and would be there till January. (Actually her father asked on her behalf.) Santa was able to assure her that he just the day before he did indeed get her letter and when he got back to the North Pole that evening he was preparing to make the special trip and visit her house before she left. Her father nodded his approval and we talked about what part of Florida were they going to? She said Sanabol Island. We talked about how the beach was one of my favorite places to take a vacation. We talked about the wonderful shells and the marvels of sea glass. Sea glass is those pieces of glass from ship wrecks that have been churned by the sea and smoothed out and look like gems, then washed up on shore. Magic! HOHOHO!!!

Brady is about 1 year old. He was terrified and never really warmed up to the stranger in the red suit. But he started to play peek-a-boo as most children do at that age do. He ran with exuberance all through the room containing the stage and many folding chairs. Then he ran around the big Christmas tree on the main floor of that wonderful old building. He was trying to entice me to chase him much like my Border collie does when he tries to get our Cocker Spaniel to play. Brady really didn't want me to catch him but the running away from the chase was new fun for him. Magic. HOHOHO!!! HOHOHO!!!

THE PERSONAL CARE HOME

Recently, the new owner of the Personal Care Home that once had provided two years of care for my Mother-in-law asked me to be Santa for their annual Christmas party. The event was like the others in that there seemed to be no real plan other than to be Santa. (I'm getting better at making these events up as I go) The loose plan was to make an appearance read something ('Twas the Night...) and give out gifts. By pre-arrangement the gifts were all ready to put into Santa's sack.

Upon arriving I sat at the first table and had a couple of cookies. The people that worked there sat at the same table and they had their children with them. Cameron age 4 was quite taken back by the prospect of sitting at the same table with Santa. It was fun to watch him be on his best behavior while the "boy" in him was busting to come out and be the "boy". As it was, he was able to procure a second candy cane before I could realize it. He kept watching me out of the corner of his eye, just to see if I was watching him. It took him a long time to smile, but he finally did. Magic! HOHOHO!!!

Showtime! I knew since the residents had just eaten, I had limited time to hand out the presents and visit with each before the urge to nap hit them. One by one, each was given a gift by Santa and we all did a bit of "visiting" It is hard to tell what challenges each resident faces as they process information. When I moved to "Sis" she started to cry. It didn't look like she was terrified, but cried she did. I gave her gift and she cried some more. I moved to all the others even delivering packages to some still in their rooms. I worked back to Sis and she cried again. She said she was so happy to see me she started crying. Magic!

My wife had found in a Chicken Soup for the Soul Christmas Spirit book the background story of the beloved poem. I read it first, then the poem and by the ending several people were crying. I have to admit that I never knew 'sugar plums' were actually prunes. As I was preparing to depart, I kept hearing from several people that I was the best...that I was the most believable... best there is that word again, best... so, humbling. I can't be the best ever.

THE SHOW MUST GO ON

Joelle was turning 8 years old on this day and her parents were throwing a combination Birthday party and Christmas party at the local performing arts theatre. There was to be a D-J cake and gifts, and an exploration of the theatre from top to bottom as only kids can do. And, of course there was Santa. Katie and I had never met as all the arrangements were made by phone. I arrived a little early since the party was held at the active community theatre. They constantly provide entertainment with the production of live plays and other entertainment.

When I arrived, Katie's father, the Judge met me. No, he is a real Judge and we know of each other. "Hello, Judge" come forth from my lips and it gave him to know that he had nothing to fear with Santa in the building. He said he would find Katie. In the meantime Brad, the owner of the theatre, joined the party so it was easy to ask if he could lead me backstage to make a truly surprise appearance for Joelle and her friends? He led me through the catacombs under the theatre. I fully expected to see the Phantom appear. We used Brad's cell phone light to guide us as he advised me several times to watch my head. I have lived long in my life and have yet to learn how to watch my head since my eyes are a part of my... Next it was watch my back going through a tight crawl space. Finally we and turned a corner and BOOM! Santa was on stage as the man behind the curtain. Magic!

On cue the D-J played "Santa Claus is coming to Town". The children clapped and yelled as the curtain opened. The lights were bright on and I was on stage. I inspected my N-N list, and then each child had my undivided attention. Joelle was the most surprised.

Joelle became the magic that day. She wanted to be certain that all of her guests got to visit with me before she did. She is probably a miniature control freak but I'm going to think of her as a stage mother, oops manager. Each child came and sat on my lap, and we discussed what was on their minds, and the nature of their behavior, and what they wanted for Christmas. This was definitely a different socio-economic class. The requests for I-Pads and I-Phones and other fancy devices far out-numbered the requests for dolls and racecars. When it was Joelle's turn, she said she wanted a sewing machine. I was quite taken back as I never had a request for a sewing machine. I asked if she knew how to sew: she said she was learning. My next question was what she was going to sew, and she told me that she wanted to help make clothes for her friends that couldn't afford to buy new clothes. I cried inside and perhaps outside as well. Magic!

PARTY TIME

Now it is time for the first home party of the season. An urgent call from Linda B.; she was desperate. She was having a Christmas party for the children and grandchildren in her family, and the man she had contracted to be Santa, couldn't. He cancelled at the last minute! Could I possibly? PLEASE! As these things go, I had to say yes. Less than 3 days... I had picked up the presents she had and purchased and placed them in Santa's Huge Toy bag. I could barely pick it up, but I did. Through the garage and into the basement to Grandmother's house we go. The children were all gathered and seemed to be waiting for something. I couldn't possibly imagine what it might be... Oh I know... In my very best Santa voice I cried out, "Merry Christmas Everybody!" With squeals of delight each child tried to match my resounding voice, and collectively they did.

After reading/reciting 'Twas the Night Before Christmas, the naughty and nice list was produced, the fun began. I called each child by name and they came to sit on my lap. We conversed about what they wanted for Christmas. Santa assured each one that if they were good, they just might see that item that will bring them some joy. The oldest girl, Gabrielle started crying and wound not come near me. She moved from mom to nana and back to mom crying. She had not been told of her position on the list but she must have felt guilty for some past infraction and she was afraid she was on the naughty list. This was confirmed by an elf in the room as he let the big guy know that she was indeed thinking she was on the naughty list. After a quick re-check and a double check Santa determined that he had her confused with Gabrielle that lived at the same address but in a different city. What a silly mistake! Santa found her name on the nice list and there was an instant change. She quit crying. She smiled. She laughed. She sat on my lap. Magic! HOHOHO!!! HOHOHO!!! HOHOHO!!!

STORY TIME 2.0, DIFFERENT TOWN

After a drive to a neighboring town I appeared as the Claus at another Library for Story time. Having barely burst through the door Santa was practically tackled by a 2 year girl. She gave me a hug and a smile. No matter what anyone says, that is better than a coke and a smile any day. (Advertising nostalgia from days long gone.) They had planned the evening, so it wasn't a make it up as you go evening. Santa would head to Santa's corner by the tree, Santa would read the same two books as the other story time and then talk to the children. (The Elf did a wonderful job of providing me with names.) Afterwards they would decorate cut-out cookies with frosting and sprinkles. It is a good thing the "Christmas Cookie Sprinkle Snitcher" returned the sprinkles! Then they were to make an ornament by sticking self-sticking foam pieces together.

Alyssa did not want to have anything to do with Santa as he sat in the chair or as he came near to her. She had blonde pigtails and she was about eighteen months old. She was quite content to decorate her own cookie without the guiding hand of mom and dad. She learned that she could "layer" frosting from a can onto a thin sugar cookie multiple times if only she took her time. And took her time she did. The frosting made the entire project about an inch tall. Covered with sprinkles it looked like a dentist's delight. HOHOHO!!!

Watching the children work on their ornaments gave me a chance to praise each and tell them what a wonderful job they had done in crafting their two ornaments. But again it was the tenacity of Alyssa that caught my eye. Sitting in the rocking chair and watching

Alyssa as she quietly, yet in a very determined manner, crafted the foam pieces together to make a beautiful ornament. With guidance from her mother, Alyssa's foam ornament soon took on a very finished look. After a little coaxing she decided to let me inspect her precious artwork. She was only willing to get within an arm's length of the big guy in the red suit, but she showed it to me before she sought her father's approval. Santa gave it back to her and her face glowed when I told her how special it was. Magic! HOHOHO!!! HOHOHO!!! HOHOHO!!!

SOMETHING TO REALLY TUG
AT YOUR HEART STRINGS

Each year a local hospital provides the food and gifts for a Christmas party for children that have parents needing food and clothing from our own Community Ministries. (This is an organization in town through the United Methodist Church that provides food and clothing bank services.) It is an angel tree project where the employees select a name and buy a gift. The gifts are then distributed by Santa. This year the event fell the day after 20 first and second graders were senselessly gunned down by a crazed murderer in a small town in Connecticut. There is a very fine line between sheltering children from the evil in the world and acknowledging at the same time that the evil exists.

Santa is doing what he does best in the midst of 50 of the poorest of the poor children in the County. Many of whom may have had to face the evil issues of abandonment or alcohol or abuse or hunger or no new clothing or not having heat in their home or apartment or drug addicted parents or who knows what else. We were there to give them a party complete with food, warmth, and a gift and try to make it as fun as possible and have cookies. We can't forget the cookies.

It was time to read my story about Rufus the bear and give Rufus the Bear away. Instead of reading the winning number outright, everyone was to raise their hands if they had the first number on the ticket. Of course everyone did. Then everyone was to keep their hands up if they had the second number. They all did. Next in the sequence waving their hands to signify they had the third number. Every hand waved. They did the same with the fourth number. All hands were still waving. When we moved to the fifth number some hands were dropped. Now there could only be ten hands still up. And, "the last the last number is a seven. Whoever has the last number "7" wins Rufus the bear!" A girl of about age 10 came forth and claimed her bear. Her name was Madison. She was carrying things in the bag on her shoulder. Hallmark movie makers could not have scripted it better. Madison won a bear with a story written by the Claus about a girl named Madison and a bear. Magic!

Joshua was there as well. He was just nine years old and oh so full of hurt. Joshua's father had been man killed in the Quad accident earlier this year. His father was a victim of an evil disease known as alcoholism. He told me his father was drunk and drove over a cliff. Joshua just looked me in the eye and cried. "I miss my father so much..." The usually unflappable big guy in the bright red suit is really struggled with the magic here. God help me! We prayed together once again. When I told him I cared, he cried. I cried as well.

LITTLE GIRLS AT LITTLE LYN'S

It's time to shift gears. My ancient hunter, gatherer wiring kicks in when visiting a store, usually moving to the exact item on my mental list, snatching it up and proceeding to the nearest cash register to pay and leave. My average time in a store to make a purchase is 2.7 minutes. In what seems to be foreign territory for a male, is the most unlikely place for Santa to sit in a chair and be available for children. However Santa did sit in the chair on two occasions...

It was the place especially for the Mothers and Grandmothers of little girls and boys. It could be called the Grandmother's Dream Children's Clothing Emporium. The store sells a large variety of everyday fairly priced clothing items for children. Because it is of excellent quality, parents and grandparents select items for everyday use. Once an item is outgrown it is stored for a sibling or passed on in some way. In addition, they sell quality special occasion clothing for both boys and girls unlike what can be found in box stores.

The frilly girl's dresses and accessories that are distinctly lacey and feminine seem to garner the most attention. Several styles are embellished with satin and lace and ribbons in styles that make adult women collectively go "oohh and aahh". This seems to be the place for some special occasion clothing that may be only worn once. When you add patent leather shoes to the mix the "oohh and aahh" effect is increased ten-fold! At this store several women join the "oohh and aahh" chorus at the same time. *It is shopping for the joy of shopping.* Each 3 or 4 year old guest brings an entourage especially selected to help pick out the very best item of clothing for that special occasion. (And of course, to help "oohh and aahh")

While there, Santa observed and discovered the secret formula known only to women. 97.5% of the time women spend shopping is spent in what women do well or best (Not wanting to get in trouble here, but, refer instead to the study quoted in the book "Why Men Don't Listen, And Why Women Can't Read Maps". The study suggested that on the average day men generally say about 3,000 words and women say about 10,000 words. You can draw your own conclusions) and it seems that 2.5% of the time is spent in the actual selection and purchase of an item.

While there Santa became acquainted with twelve girls and one boy. There were also twenty seven adult women and two tag-a-long men whose sole job was to hold the purses. The twelve girls were mostly willing to sit and talk with Santa. But that lone boy seemed to sense that he was a boy in enemy territory. Perhaps it was his camo clothing and the bandana that gave him away. Actually he was very friendly and was the one who convinced several of the girls that it was okay to sit on Santa's lap. Perhaps he sensed that we were of the band of brothers trapped behind enemy lines. Magic! HOHOHO!!! HOHOHO!!! HOHOHO!!!

IT'S PARTY TIME AGAIN

Since the Claus had been to Chuck and Susan's home before, nervousness was not an issue this time around. It has been an entire year and here at the same home where Santa made his first home party appearance. This family has 4 "Chucks" in the current family tree and every time someone called out (my name) Chuck, not turning was difficult. It was difficult to remember to stay in character.

The adults were in place and the children were all poised for the visit from the big guy. Having dropped off the big Santa toy bag a day earlier it would be filled to capacity. While in full Santa mode and having the full bag slung over my shoulder I burst through the front door and "really totally scared" several of the children by shouting "Merry Christmas". We started bantering quickly as Santa was far more familiar with the family and the children. Lots and lots of laughter. HOHOHO!!!

'Twas the night… and then give the gifts to the children. When they were all distributed Santa said "you can only open the presents when Santa yells, 'open your presents'". It was more difficult to hold back these eager children then to hold back the reins on the reindeer Christmas Eve. Again a delayed count increased the anticipation… "One, two, on you mark, set, eighty seven, open your presents!" In an instant flying paper made the room look like a parade down hero's canyon. We did a similar thing with the cookies as we proceeded through the ritual to eat a cookie with Santa.

This year the family was more comfortable with me. They also knew there wouldn't object a picture or two or sixty-three being taken with the all children and family members and Grandmamma. As she came to sit on my knee a chorus of concerned family members shouted out, "Be careful of her back!" knowing how fragile older folks are I was very careful. Then she admitted to all that her naughty side caused her to be responsible for the entire brood. "OH MY! Grandmamma, whatever, do you mean?" Laughter and more Laughter. "HOHOHO!!! HOHOHO!!! HOHOHO!!! HOHOHO!!! HOHOHO!!! HOHOHO!!!

Story recited, gifts distributed, laughter, Photos taken memories preserved on a film or electronically, Lots of laughter. More laughter as I prepared to depart. Landon, who had skirted around the room all evening to avoid me, brought me a cookie. In his bravest voice he held out the prized gift and said, "Here, this for you." Magic!

DAY CARE #1

Central scheduling seems to have made an error. I kept looking at my calendar and saw my next appearance date was at Echo day care on Tuesday the 18th. The mind that was once like a steel trap has recently let some things slip through like opening the flood gates. But the date seemed wrong. The 17th kept creeping through and haunting me. On the 17th we slept in late and in the middle of our devotional I told my wife I have to verify the date. When I called sure enough it was the 17th. It was unfortunate but it was necessary to inform them I would be 15 minutes late. I take full responsibility for the mistake. Now we dashed through the prep process and Santa was out the door... This daycare is a secular company using the church's property.

Moving through the halls of the church and ringing the sleigh bells it was very easy to hear the anticipation. Most adults here it as noisy children but Santa hears it as magic! They were so surprised to see a big man in a red suit. Three children ran to hug me. The jumping and clapping and smiles were music to my ears. Having been directed to the special rocking chair that was to mine for the next hour the fun began. This was another unscripted event so deciding to read about the "Christmas Cookie Sprinkle Snitcher" was an easy choice. One girl yelled out that I had read it at the library.

Upon seeking her permission to share that wonderful story with her classmates, she gave her approval and they listened to the story about the rascal Snitcher. Catching my breath after reading was a good thing since the children were going to sing a song they had learned, there is no way that could be refused. "Up on the Housetop..." (Then for my part ...HOHOHO... HOHOHO!) Oh there was such glee from children. The song has places to sing got to do it again in the course of the song to the delight of the children. "'Twas the night… was next. We distributed the presents and when I said reindeer they all opened their gifts. Then it was time to have a cookie with Santa and I made sure none started eating until I said plum pudding. The countdown began and finally "plum pudding".

As we were enjoying the decorated sugar cookies together, a boy from the center of the group came up to me. He said he had to tell me something about someone else sitting next to him in the crowd. I tried to caution him by saying it wasn't nice to tell on other children. He pointed to another boy and said "He really can't cry". I had to let this percolate a moment before I could process what he had just said. It finally hit all the synapses, and it clicked. He was so concerned about his friend that he felt it was something Santa should know. Magic! HOHOHO!!!

DAY CARE #2

Echo day care, same name of the Day Care two days ago, different city. They were renting a commercial building. The children all had the quick and easy three dimensional Santa hat complete with cotton ball tassel and name badges. Thanks to Judy from another location. As soon as I moved through the door and said "Merry Christmas" all the children instantly jumped up and moved in my direction. Not quite! It was a stunned surprise. It was a moment or two before the wheels clicked in and they realized I was Santa and he was there to visit them. HOHOHO!!! Collectively they all got it at the same moment. Within seconds I was practically gang tackled by a group of children ages three and four.

Santa read about the Sprinkle Snitcher and then the story about the Night Before...but it would seem a monster has been created, the ritual of eating cookies with Santa. It is like tea time in Japan where the ritual of drinking tea is solely for the pure pleasure of drinking tea. We were all sitting and waiting to be offered a cookie. Parents had provided several kinds of cookies and the next thing I knew everyone was being offered one kind of cookie then another then another. Santa had three before he knew what hit his plate and he was to lead the eating of the cookies. When Santa says "eat cookies" then you all can eat your cookies. One... two...ready... set... pumpkin butter... eighty seven... eat cookies.

Gifts for each child, call them up one by one... they each came and sat on my lap. Without a doubt photos were taken but there were no flashes. Oh modern technology at it very finest. Hallie ask me how Santa knew her name. Just, as predicted, a 3D Santa complete with name plates worked like a charm. It is just like when you go to Wal-Mart and Katie wants to know I knew her name that is on her name badge. Austin was the best when he asked how many reindeer came with me today. My response was that we only bring two trainee reindeer so we can rest the other reindeer for the big night. The impressed was passed on them all that Vixen loves carrots. While preparing to leave Seth ran to Santa and hugged as strong as any 3 year old can do and said "I love you Santa" Once one child hugged Santa, every child knew it was okay and they couldn't wait to get in line and hug me. All their precious hugs were so sincere and real gave the feeling of real magic! HO HO HO!!! HO HO HO!!! HO HO HO!!!

DAY CARE #3

A privately run day care in a church in a town 30 miles away was the setting for the next group of children. After arriving, I go through my checklist – go over the working plan with the organizing mothers, Start ringing the sleigh bells, trek up the stairs, brace for the onslaught of little bodies trying to gang tackle the Claus. Tackled!!! Almost. It doesn't get any better than that. The church-run day care children are generally better behaved, but children are children. They stand in awe and wonder, and as children they expect to have childlike experiences.

The plan, was to enter the Sanctuary, sit in the big chair, and have the group of children sit or kneel around me and take pictures. Suddenly I felt very uncomfortable, because all of my life I have been taught that men don't wear hats into church. Here Santa was, with his red Santa hat on walking into church. The good news -- lightning did not strike, but tempting God wasn't my style. And if my memory serves correctly, St. Nicholas was a Bishop and wore the red cassock and red MITRE' hat. (One of the theories is that Santa's suit seems to be red for that very reason.)

The first stop was to say a prayer upon entering the Sanctuary, something that took my guide back. The move to the chair was in some way the trigger to flinging open the church doors open with the eager anticipation that only little children can provide. Each child ran to me sat in my lap had photo a taken and made room for the next one. It was magical. The group photo was taken. Next it was time to read about the Sprinkle Snitcher. They all sat and listened. After story time, everyone was to wash their hands and head off to the basement to decorate Christmas Cookies.

Clean hands were a prerequisite for sharing a cookie with Santa. Just imagining the scene in the washroom as the kids hurried to wash their hands makes me smile. Santa occupied the chair in the middle of the table. They rushed to the table to see who could sit the nearest to the man in the red suit. One boy had his chair picked out and he planned a route that required the most steps. His planning in advance allowed him to sit next to me with the biggest smile you have ever seen. Magic! All the others found their places in a quiet orderly fashion. Sure they did! HOHOHO!!!

We were each given a cookie, and then it was time to frost and sprinkle the cookies. All went well with one exception. The sprinkles poured out of the jar faster than the decorators were ready to handle. Santa saved the moment by showing them a little trick that his mother taught him when he was their age. If you lick your fingers then touch them to the extra sprinkles on the plate, the sprinkles would stick to your fingers and you could lick them off. Each tried the technique, and faces glowed with the "secret" knowledge that Santa provided. They all looked like they were getting away with something. Magic! Once again retelling the story about "The Night..." was the order of the day. Then came the best part of the visit: each child ran to me and hugged me one last time. It was truly a very Merry Christmas gathering.

SOMETHING MORE TO TUG
AT THE HEART STRINGS

Recently, Special Needed Magic happened. This year the honor fell to me again. I am so humbled by this experience. The list the teacher e-mailed the following information: "We have bought the children pajamas and sweatpants and a sweatshirt or t-shirts to match the sweat pants. The dollar store is a great place to start... the play money, books and puzzles are great and only $1. We just bought them all coats, ball caps and winter hats so they are good with that. I only have 1 girl this year."

- Boy #1–doesn't talk much, however, he loves reading books... he reads on a second grade level, he loves music (Christmas and children's) he likes videos... Scooby doo, Barney and the Wiggles, he loves basketball and he swims. (his parents are involved)
- Boy #2–Likes John Deere tractors and puzzles. He likes football. He can't read at all. (He is in boys scouts, his mom is involved)
- Boy #3–can read books on a second grade level. He likes movies, perhaps Avatar? Big farm tractors... and John Deere items too. (He lives on a farm)
- Boy #4–Likes Army men, army tanks, cologne (he does not have any parents, but is raised by his grandma)
- Boy #5–Barney tapes, wrestling men, he needs a backpack, socks, and a watch... he has nothing (He comes from very poor home)

- Boy #6–Likes wrestling men, match box cars, tooth brush, deodorant, he wants underwear, and a watch? Yea, I know, boxers size small in men's this boy doesn't wear underwear because he doesn't have any to wear. He is working on hygiene issues. (Comes from very poor home)
- Boy #7–He wants lead pencils, jeans size 10-12 or sweatpants He has nothing and often wears pants way too small. (He comes from very poor home, only mom, no dad)
- Boy #8–pants size 28/30, listens to country music on CD's. He would like a watch, and a belt. (Dad works out of town and he was a life skills student as well at one time)
- Boy #9–He would like a shirt, size medium men's, socks, cards and watch and cologne.
- Girl #10 – She would like a basketball or soccer ball, shirts size 14, hair things and bracelets (she has no parents, both died and gram raises her)

How do you tackle a list like that? I understand being poor and how devastating that situation is in the lives of children. Then, one has to ask are they developmentally slow because they are poor. Or, is it because they only have one or often no parents? Or have they become victims of some terrible malady such as poor neonatal care, fetal alcohol syndrome, parents that used drugs or smoked during the pregnancy? Or were they victims of physical abuse? What, a can of worms this could be.

These are children in teenage bodies that can't read. These are children in teenage bodies that don't know about brushing their teeth and other hygiene issues. These are children in teenage bodies that never held a football or a basketball, or played with a remote control car. How do you begin to make it special for children that don't seem to have had a childhood?

To me it was important to do my best to allow them a chance to be a child again. If someone liked basketball or football or soccer they should get the ball for that sport. If someone liked farm tractors they should get a tractor. Army tanks, how about a remote control car? If one needed a backpack and socks that is what they should get.

If a child doesn't wear underwear because he doesn't have any, guess what he is getting, and it is not his two front teeth. It is the same with jeans and watches and socks. How can they be kids when they don't even have clothing to wear to let them be children?

One boy, a participant from last year, recognized me as being the same Santa from the year before. I told him I remembered him as my Rudolf replacement and was wondering why he never showed up for training. He laughed and so did all the others. We distributed the gifts that were again paid for by the local Rotary Club. Two of the children, one boy and one girl, could not attend for whatever reason, one boy and the girl. So here was Santa, with just the boys and the teachers. I knew that I could joke just a little differently with just boys so I did. To the boy receiving 10 pair of boxer shorts I reminded him he should only wear one pair at a time. I told him the girls weren't any more impressed if they saw three pair exposed because of his droopy pants. Genuine boy laughter. I showed the boy who held a football for the first time how to hold the ball so it would fly straight and not look like a wounded duck. Genuine boy laughter. To the two boys who now had spray cologne we joked about how the girls would now chase them like they do in the TV commercials and they should be careful how they use the stuff. Genuine boy laughter. Magic! We took a group photos using several cameras.

We were going to give away another Rufus the bear that needed a special home. After they went through the anguish of each of seven numbers on the drawing ticket the put-away bear went to the smallest boy there. Magic! He promised to give Rufus a good home. HO HO HO!!! HO HO HO!!! HO HO HO!!!

THE BLING THING PLACE

From 11:00 AM till 2:00 PM Santa sat in the chair waiting for the children to arrive. Even though today was the last big-weekend shopping day before Christmas, business was slow in the store. It had snowed just enough to make people think twice about venturing out. According to widely-circulated rumors, the world was supposed to have ended on Friday. Some people may have been too stressed to shop. And, I suspect that people had made most of their big purchases before today even hit the calendar, there were fewer procrastinators out shopping. Most of the shoppers were men searching for that special gift that would endear them to their spouse or girlfriend.

I was to sit in the chair, greet the guests, and be available to all the children. Ready and willing to fulfill those requirements, I began the wait. For the entire three hours only seven children showed up, including a set of twins that arrived as Santa was packing up to head back. Ann and Hallie, age 8 in the 4th grade, condescended to sit on the lap and talk to the big guy.

I had gone outside several times and close to 87 cars honked their horns as their passengers waved and smiled. Since it was freezing outside I guessed that the several cars driving by with a rear window open did so to allow a child to see Santa. I did my absolute best to make eye contact with every person I could under the age 10. The smiles were incredible.

While outside, I did my best to entice passersby to enter the store, but very few actually stopped. Suddenly a person nearly went flying through the windshield as car came to a screeching halt. A woman jumped out of the car, ran to me, and proceeded to hand me a can of Diet Coke. I was quite taken back at the entire exchange. I said, "Yes, I truly would." She was a person that had lost 100 pounds and wanted to explain how. Okay, what's the catch?

What is her secret? Reduce carbs. Been there, done that. Lost 65 pounds and when I went off the diet I gained 75 pounds back. I didn't have the heart to tell her. She was a weight loss zealot much like someone who has quit smoking becomes a relenting crusader against other smokers. The woman asked if someone could take her photo with Santa. That was why we were there. We went into the store and found someone to snap the photo. Then in a flash she was gone. One might have thought it was a dream; it was over that quickly. But at that moment in time that person created magic with her heart and her smile which were as big and as delightful as that of any seven year old. HOHOHO!!! Besides I still had the diet coke in hand.

A TRUE FIRST... THE BEAUTY PAGEANT

Another very loosely designed plan was to place me at the theatre to crown the winning beauty contestants competing in several categories. At 4:00PM. I'm not sure who planned this event for the Saturday before Christmas but not for me to reason why. I waited in the parking lot until the agreed time of 3:45 and then headed in for the crowning of the winners.

Forty-seven girls in different age groups competed on this day; many in dresses they would only wear once in their lives. There were young girls who that were just learning to walk with graceful poise, wearing high heels which made them more wobbly. Since beauty pageants had never been part of my realm, I didn't have a clue as to how they were judged. Luckily, my job was to present myself on stage and crown the winners. Just as live TV seldom goes as planned, neither does a live pageant. By the time I was in place to crown the winner, the winners had already been crowned. No longer needed, I planned to escape quickly, but the organizer spotted me and said I was to go on stage anyway to wish everyone a Merry Christmas. By the time I moved into position my sense of smell was assaulted by thirty-five different colognes. Olfactory overload is definitely not my thing so after a quick "Merry Christmas everybody and a special congratulations to all the winners." I was out of there.

My exit took me past the room where five unsuccessful contestants were also preparing to leave early. Since the finalists were still on stage, I made a special stop in the room to encourage them to keep on trying and maybe someday they too would be winners.

Each girl made it a point to hug me. One of the early departing participants hugged me and, said with insight way beyond her years, "I know that you can't always get what you want. But you and Jesus know what is best for me, and that is what I will get from you this Christmas. Thank you!" Magic! Santa cried again. Magic!

My neighbor from across the street sought me out a few days later and told me that I was the best Santa ever. Her daughter was in the pageant and Kelly was so proud of both her daughter and the best Santa was her neighbor. There is that word best again.

15 MINUTES OF FAME

Andy Warhol once said that everyone would at some time in their lives experience 15 minutes of fame. Or perhaps infamy. My fifteen minutes might have happened. Recently a reporter for a local newspaper was completing a story on a non-profit organization where Santa was volunteering. During the course of her gathering information for her story, she remarked that I looked like I could be Santa.

Since it comes from deep in the diaphragm, it is necessary to occasionally practice the HO! HO! HO! And this was one of those times. She remarked that it was wonderful. She received my Santa business card. And, so much for that fleeting moment! Soon she was gone and nothing more about the conversation. Until...

She called the number on my business card about six months later. On that early December day she identified herself as the reporter that was at the Ministry earlier this year. the natural assumption was that she was calling to schedule a gig or something like that. It took me several moments to recover when she said she wanted to shadow me off and on for a week as Santa. Knowing where the reindeer poop falls, I directed the conversation to include my wife. Then she said she had been given the assignment to write a story about Santa. She wanted to know about the preparation, and the presentation.

Thinking a graceful exit would not be possible the agreed time was set. She came to the house and watched as the preparations progressed. She photographed the beard whitening process, the placement of the suspenders and even how the boot covers slid over the top of the Santa suit pants. Over the next week we were everywhere together. We went to the Library, the Special Needs Class and even to a home party. She photographed and filmed everything the big guy did. Trying to act and be normal is very difficult when everything you do and say is being recorded, cautious and guarded moments rule the day.

The climax of the week was the recording of an interview about the how and whys of being Santa. We parted company and the next day a photo of a boy aged three tugging at my beard appeared on the front page of the newspaper. Thinking the process was over it wasn't thought about again. Perhaps the Editor had a more important story to cover. For ten days it had become just another event in the life of...

Sunday morning there it was, on the front page on the top of the fold a photo and story about Becoming Santa. The person once so reluctant to even put on the suit had made front page news. That place seemingly reserved for the reporting of fires and murders and corrupt politicians. I was not only on the front page but the article filled the back page of the front section. Six photos and a very complimentary, positive presentation of Santa. The video has garnered over 30,000 views on You Tube: Becoming Santa- Chuck Hubbell. Virginia, there is a Santa Claus.

A year later Santa Claus captured the imagination of Mary Dreliszak a Blog writer on People who inspire. I was greatly humbled by the kind words she wrote about Santa. A great deal of the humility comes from the other famous and semi-famous people she has chosen to highlight over the past few years.

CANCELLING CHRISTMAS

Aunt Bev had booked an appearance for a party on the Sunday before Christmas. It would be a surprise visit for three boys ages 8, 7 and 5. All preparations were made for a normal Santa visit. However about an hour before the scheduled time the Aunt made a desperate call saying we had a problem. Mom was going to cancel Christmas. She was at her wits end as she had three boys that could not keep their toys of the floors in their bedrooms.

At the appointed time, the not so jolly elf banged on the front door as loud as possible. Two boys answered the door. Looking angry and upset, it was easy to dredge the angriest voice possible. Bellowing out that I had to make an emergency stop at this house because we were going to cancel Christmas. I had heard that three boys couldn't keep their toys off their bedroom floors. Do you boys have any idea how many children all over the world are going to be upset because we have to cancel Christmas?"

Nicholas the five year old darted to his room without having his feet touch the floor. And, I laughed in spite of myself. The other two boys were less conspicuous about the urgency but, they also went quickly to their rooms.

After about five minutes kibitzing with the adults, Nicky came and grabbed my hand. He wanted to show me how good his room looked without any toys on the floor. Since he was pulling my hand, we went to his room. It was impressive, he had made a wonderful effort in removing all the toys from the floor. He needed reassuring and he got bunches. However, it was noted that it would be necessary to chastise the parents for making him sleep on such an uncomfortable and lumpy bed. The other two boys had used the extra time to finish their rooms, which were remarkably clear of stuff on the floor.

We read, "'Twas the Night…" and it was time to visit with the boys. To see if they had been good or bad and ask what they wanted for Christmas. The highlight of the afternoon was when asked, Nicky said quite loudly and proudly that he wanted a baby sister. Assuming the mother was pregnant turned out to be incorrect. Everyone laughed and twitter pated. He got my best efforts to dissuade him from wanting a baby sister. He was relentless. Six months later it was learned that mom was indeed with child, due a week before Christmas… a girl. The family, Mrs. Claus and believers in Magic everywhere, were relieved that we had been on vacation nine months prior.

The most beautiful girl was born two months pre-mature and weighed only three and a half pounds. By the time came for me to hold this Santa Baby she had grown to a whopping five and a half pounds.

The next time Nicky sits on the big guy's lap, he is getting reminded to be very, very careful about what he asks for next time. HO! HO! HO!

KNOCK, KNOCK, KNOCKING ON HEAVEN'S DOOR

Several years are now under the wide belt with the big buckle. Perhaps I should say "Been there, done that." Perhaps I find something else to do. Maybe the magic doesn't really exist anymore…

To be sure, I was dog tired. The day was long and I had completed a range of gigs. First thing in the morning it was a visit at a retailer, then it was a party and toy give away for less fortunate children of the community. A visit to a group home for much older Down's syndrome men, was followed by Santa posing for several pictures with the Stanley Cup and then dropping the puck at a minor league hockey game. The day climaxed with a private party with about twenty children.

It was only nine o'clock in the evening and it was time to drive to the house, divest myself of the red suit and boots, take a shower and relax. I had been home just enough time to remove the hat, unfasten the belt and unzip the fur coat. The phone rang and every tired fiber of my being told me not to answer that constant ringing. My wife gave me those pleading, "don't answer it" looks. Anyone that is married can testify to that look. Caller ID was no help…

With all the courage I could muster I answered just in the "Nick" of time. The voice on the other end identified herself and I knew I had nothing to fear. She owned the retail shop for the first gig of the day. She asked if I still had on my Santa suit. Before I could answer she told me to meet her at Wendy's in five minutes… she would explain everything then. My vehicle was faster than hers and I had just gotten out of my car to see if I could locate hers.

She pulled in behind my car and said "follow me we are just going three blocks" and she would it explain it all when we got there. She was correct, it was three blocks. She parked and I eased my vehicle behind hers. "We are going to Grandma Jean's house. Jerry and Lisa had just arrived after driving three hours. They have their two children with them, Josh age seven and Madison age five. She went on to say, "Josh wants a Skylander tow toy and Madison wants a 'Frozen Castle'"

The first time ever this year found me in Toys R Us to check out all the new and different and very desired toys. My market research paid off several times this year but never so much as it did tonight. I knew exactly what they wanted and was going to catch them off guard and create magic.

Before I was told to burst in the door I was fed another piece of information, "They will all be in the living room and just so you know Grandma Jean is in a bed in the living room also." Before I could react she pushed me through the door and said, "do your thing."

In the blink of an eye, it was necessary to process everything I was seeing and trying to comprehend. I have been there before. I have seen it before. It was unspoken but it was there. The bedside potty chair, the walker and the look on Grandma Jean's face spoke volumes. She was clearly facing her last days. Her son Jerry and his bride Lisa had just driven to get there perhaps just in time. Josh and Madison needed some Christmas magic from Santa. I called them each by name and the glow of magic started. Finding a chair I sat down and started talking to Josh and Madison. I asked how they liked their trip. And if they were tired.

Time to get down to business. Before each could say what they wanted, the big guy in the red suit told each what he had heard from the special elves who were really paying close attention to them as they might have to be away from home for Christmas and with no notice at all. Oh My! The magic was lighting up the dimly lit room. After we discussed what all they thought wanted for Christmas, Madison became a little more animated. She said she wanted Grandma Jean to get better. Then I was humbled. She asked, "how did I know how to find them?" I replied with the only thing I could think of at the time,

"Cookie dust." It was reassuring to them that I had known that they each had a cookie that day and the dust followed them. It was a very lucky but educated guess that worked.

I never want to exclude elderly people from the festivities and I leaned over to Grandma Jean's face, and heard her faintly say, "I see Santa and I see Jesus…"

Jerry encouraged Josh to give a tug on my beard and Lisa whispered into Madison's ear. Madison wanted to know who gave Santa a gift for Christmas and I assured her that the elves and Mrs. Claus had presents waiting for me on Christmas day. She said she was going to make something special for me since I had taken time from the North Pole to see Grandma Jean before she died…

HEARING CLEARLY
WITH NEW EYES

As the journey develops, striving to be a better Santa Claus includes studying how other people hone their craft. After reading a story about a deaf girl that had made to visit a Santa. She felt excluded because he could not understand the language she spoke with her hands. It hit like a ton of bricks. Hearing impaired children feel excluded when they can't communicate with the man in red. In fact the hearing impaired community has the perception that Santa is only for normal children.

After reading this, it became apparent that hearing impaired children should at a minimum have someone to interpret for Santa. The elves and I decided that a remedy was needed. It did not take long. An angel from heaven appeared. Cindy was not only the answer to the communication dilemma but she was a genuine "twofer". Not only was she willing to interpret for Santa she was willing to be the elf as well. She taught Santa how to sign HO HO HO.

We worked together most of the day. The visits were normal and uneventful. Perhaps this was much ado about nothing. Then Elf Cindy presented a girl whose parents were both hearing impaired while Mary Ann the eight year old had normal hearing. Children often whisper things in Santa's ear to test the mettle of the big guy. (They wonder if they are going to get what they asked for in secret) Most parents try hard and listen to the secret things children tell Santa. Mary Ann whispered to me what she wanted for Christmas and a miracle occurred. Cindy signed the request. No words were spoken to the parents. They were unable to hear what she requested, but, they now knew for the first time what their daughter had secretly asked of Santa. Because Santa had big tears in his eyes… It was time to "feed the reindeer" Magic!

LIFE ALTERING REFLECTIONS

Normally, when people visit a child in the hospital they provide a gift the child can hold on to or look at or play with. Often friends and family give something like a teddy bear or a toy or a game. Then in the course of events, all subsequent visitors talk about the bear and how special it is and how lucky the child is to have the bear or game etc.

Many years ago, I was a participant in a service project at Children's Hospital in Washington, D.C. The service project was to create and hand out over 400 "Happy Hats." These happy hats were for the children being treated in the hospital that day. It is a long story and many, many people participated. Each person had a job. I was not very good with scissors or a sewing machine. Nor was I willing to learn on such short notice. So, I selfishly took the best job. I got to hold the hand-held mirror up to each child and help them see how good they looked in their new hat.

This time it wasn't about a bear or a new game, it was about them and how they looked. The children there that day were afflicted with a myriad of diseases and many suffered not only the physical effects of the disease but also the effects of the treatment to cure the disease. Many children, knew their looks had been altered and not necessarily for the better. The hat was theirs and no one could take it from them. And most importantly they looked good in their hats and I was given the privilege to help them see that inner and outer beauty. It was so special to see smile after smile light up the grand hall. My life has been forever altered for the better because children could wear happy hats and the Magic shone about them.

As I don the red apparel, and whiten the beard, the mindset of creating magic kicks into overdrive. If children can establish that the man in the red suit is real, then magic is created and their self-worth is magnified. I try to spend my time listening to each child and making each one feel important even though some may not think they are. When the Claus knows their names, they believe in the magic, if only for a moment. Combine knowing their names with the listening to what they say, they feel they have value and they all feel oh, so very special!

I have learned that for most children the act of sitting on Santa's lap and having a photo taken is not why they visit with Santa. It isn't the gifts that they ask for nor is it the gift they may receive that makes their moments special. It is not the candy cane. It is something far deeper. It is as though I am holding a mirror to each child and saying to them "you are beautiful, don't you look good in your happy hat?" I want every child to have a happy hat and believe in the Magic. When I am the Claus each child receives their happy hat. And their smiles light up the room.

I was raised with the axiom, "it is better to give than receive." I have spent my life as a giver. And I haven't ever thought much about being on the receiving end of anything. The implication is that I would be rewarded somehow, someway when I least expected it. (Waiting for Candid Camera, perhaps?)

But, I can honestly admit, that I have been given a gift far beyond any material, reward. In the past few years my life has changed in a very different way than I could have possibly thought it would. I have seen life through the eyes and hearts of children. I have been humbled many more times than I can count by the innocence of children. Children who can see the magic in something most of their friends tell them doesn't exist.

I have been told I am the best. Something I know isn't true. I am not the best ever and I never will be. God is still molding his creation in me. He doesn't make junk. I am still a work in progress, but becoming Santa has been a life-changing experience for me. And the best part is the journey continues…

BREAKING LAWS

Scientists have calculated by all rules of physics and aerodynamics that bumble bees cannot possibly fly. Their weight is too heavy for their wings. Their wings are too small. Their wings cannot flap fast enough etc. But, since they can't read, they fly anyway! Magic!

1. Flying Reindeer; No known species of reindeer can fly. BUT there are 300,000 species of living organisms yet to be classified, and while most of these are insects and germs, this does not COMPLETELY rule out flying reindeer, which only Santa has ever seen.

2. Children; There are 2 billion children (persons under 18) in the world. BUT Santa doesn't (appear) to handle the Muslim, Hindu, Jewish and Buddhist children, that reduces the workload to 15% of the total… 378 million according to Population Reference Bureau. At an average (census) rate of 3.5 children per household, that's 91.8 million homes. One presumes there's at least one good child in each.

3. Timing; Santa has 31 hours of Christmas to work with, thanks to the different time zones and the rotation of the earth, assuming he travels east to west (which seems logical). This works out to 822.6 visits per second. This is to say that for each believing household with good children, Santa has less than 1/1,000th of a second to park, hop out of the sleigh, jump down the chimney, fill the stockings, distribute the remaining presents under the tree, eat whatever snacks have been left, get back up the chimney,

get back into the sleigh and move on to the next house. Assuming that each of these 91.8 million stops are evenly distributed around the earth (which, of course, we know to be false but for the purposes of our calculations we will accept), we are now talking about .78 miles per household, a total trip of 75-1/2 million miles, not counting stops to do what most of us must do at least once every 31 hours, plus feeding and etc. This means that Santa's sleigh is moving at 650 miles per second, 3,000 times the speed of sound. For purposes of comparison, the fastest man-made vehicle on earth, the Ulysses space probe, moves at a poky 27.4 miles per second- a conventional reindeer can run, tops, 15 miles per hour. (See point #1)

4. Weight; the payload on the sleigh adds another interesting element. Assuming that each child gets nothing more than a medium-sized Lego set (2 pounds), the sleigh is carrying 321,300 tons, not counting Santa, who is invariably described as overweight. On land, conventional reindeer can pull no more than 300 pounds. Even granting that "flying reindeer" (see point #1) could pull TEN TIMES the load of a normal reindeer, the job cannot be completed with just with eight, or even nine. We need 214,200 reindeer. This increases the payload–not even counting the weight of the sleigh -- to 353,430 tons. Again, for comparison -- this is four times the weight of the Queen Elizabeth.

5. Speed; 353,000 tons traveling at 650 miles per second creates enormous air resistance. This will heat the reindeer up in the same fashion as space craft re-entering the earth's atmosphere. The lead pair of reindeer will absorb 14.3 QUINTILLION joules of energy. Per second. Each. In short, they will burst into flame almost instantaneously, exposing the reindeer behind them, and create deafening sonic booms in their wake. The entire reindeer team will be vaporized within 4.26 thousandths of a second. Santa, meanwhile, will be subjected to centrifugal forces 17,500.06

times greater than gravity. A 250-pound Santa (which seems ludicrously slim) would be pinned to the back of his sleigh by 4,315,015 pounds of force. (See point #1)

By every known law of aerodynamics and physics Santa can't possibly do what he does… Yet he does! Magic! HO HO HO!!! HO HO HO!!! HO HO HO!!!

THE JOURNEY CONTINUES...

THE SECOND PART: REAL LIFE, RELIGION AND SANTA

CHRISTMAS IS...

It has been described in song, "As the most wonderful time of the year." Because…

"Then the angel said to them Do not be afraid, for behold, I bring you good tidings of great joy which will be for ALL people." Luke 2:10

THE BINGE

In the early twenty first century, customs and ideas have become topsy-turvy. For a very long time, the idea of preparing for Christmas including decorations, music and worship was put on the back burner until the day after Thanksgiving. (Even today some churches do not allow their congregations to sing Christmas carols before Christmas day). Then it is "let the shopping games begin" as the call of the season.

Retailers struggled most of the year only to discover that their sales boomed the day after Thanksgiving allowing them to show a potential profit for the year. Retailers then started pushing their merchandise via sales and several other marketing methods. At that point the gift buying season would begin in earnest. "Black Friday" madness was born.

The retailing focus changed from the Christmas gift buying binge that began after a day of football and the grand Thanksgiving meal. Now it is widely thought that maybe a day or days or even months prior to Thanksgiving will boost the bottom line. At midnight Thanksgiving night the flag drops as unbelievable prices are slapped on merchandise to entice gift givers. Today retailers even forgo the big meal and the football games and offer deep discounts starting at noon or earlier on Thanksgiving Day.

Decorations and lights once enhanced the "It's beginning to look a lot like Christmas" feeling. Today the calendar is blurred by the "Black Friday" savings touted all year long; the "Christmas in July" events appear regularly to promote cheap prices for potential gift giving. In early September, Halloween decorations that rival the gaudiest Christmas decoration displays are in place. The day after Halloween is now the official day for Christmas light displays. This further blurs the lines about exactly what and when are we celebrating.

ALL ABOARD!

The first part of this book concluded with a promise of a continuing journey... A journey that has changed me in more ways than one could possibly anticipate. The journey still moves through the realm of creating magic with children. It is more about how God has allowed his servant to grow with the talents He has given me. It is about how Our Father in heaven has created magic in and through me.

Every year it is overwhelming to see the number of requests for Santa visits grow. At the same time more children have found solace and comfort in sharing laughter, secrets and joy with the big guy in the red suit.

Each event starts out with someone having some idea how the event should go. Some people try to micro-manage the event even to the point of dictating exactly what should be said. After ten years, the best advice is to listen to the children and ignore the adults.

The Claus has grown personally in so many ways by visiting with children of all ages. It is no wonder that the Gospels of Matthew: "Assuredly, I say to you, unless you are converted and become as little children, you will by no means enter the kingdom of heaven. Therefore whoever humbles himself as this little child is the greatest in the kingdom of heaven. Whoever receives one little child like this in My name receives Me." (18:3-6); and "Let the little children come to Me, and do not forbid them; for of such is the kingdom of God. Mark." (10:14) and: "let the little children come unto me and Luke." (18:16).

My belief window has been expanded from a myopic look at the world of children to the biggest brightest panoramic view of the horizon one could imagine. At the same time my own human limitations keep restricting the view. Although "the Claus" is always seeking to become the best Santa possible, it doesn't take much introspection to know that is an impossible goal. The Claus continues to attempt to be the best. At the same time, the edge of the horizon is ever changing.

GOING BACK TO SCHOOL

In the quest to become the "best" Santa possible and at the same time maintain the Christian heritage of St. Nicholas, Santa sought enrollment in the St. Nicholas Institute. This retreat for Santas, Mrs. Claus' and aspiring St. Nicholas want-to-bees is limited to 24 people. It was very rewarding to be accepted into the class. The first of four times of attending this retreat, I was nervous and apprehensive. I felt like a baby polar bear at the North Pole.

We did not learn the mechanics of being Santa or how to promote ourselves. But rather, how to finesse our experiences with children. We learned more about St. Nicholas with our different brothers and sisters attending each year. Each has their reasons for attending and or returning. Knowing what to expect and checking our egos at the door on subsequent visits resulted in time passing far too quickly.

The invitation to attend this retreat was also extended to the Santa from Radio City Music Hall in New York City, The Santa from Atlanta, Ga., who is the current face of Santa for the Coca-Cola commercials, The Santa from Santa Claus, Indiana and twenty others from California to Florida and from Texas to Michigan.

The seminar held in October is a wonderful event culminating in an awards banquet. Within a breath-taking atmosphere of the Academy Awards, Santas are honored as the awards are given. Other honorees are those persons that best exemplify the Spirit of Christmas.

In addition to the facilitators teaching the class about St. Nicholas, we were blessed to have a former wig and make-up specialist from Disney World in Florida, a non-hearing Catholic priest that taught "hearing" Santas basic sign language, and a representative from the

Charles Schultz museum in California. (It was the 50th anniversary of "It's a Charlie Brown Christmas"). We were honored to have as a speaker, the woman that had played Zuzu in it's a "Wonderful life"

St. Nicholas is an honored icon more in the Eastern Orthodox traditions of Christianity. Learning about St. Nicholas helps to understand the roots of Santa Claus as well as the traditions of the guy in the red suit. These images include those by Conde Nast and C. Clement Moore and the Coca-Cola bottling company.

The retreat amounts to four days of intense immersion into the culture and lore of the patron Saint of Orphans, Pawnbrokers, Prisoners, Prostitutes and most oppressed people.

In a culture not known for giving to others, St. Nicholas gave. He is widely known as a person that gave away a large portion of his inherited wealth to others. He is most noted for the gold coins he anonymously gave to the daughters of a poor man so their dowries would be complete.

He became a Bishop at age 17 and he was widely thought to have attended the Council of Nicaea, where the Nicene creed was decided upon. It is safe to say that he had a temper and at that same council disagreed so strongly with another Bishop that Nicholas is rumored to have hit him with his fist.

His travels both alive and dead somewhat mirrored those of the one called Paul of Tarsus. His bones often were sought after relics for sale and were stolen and transported at least once.

A common bond forms as the band of brothers and sisters all seek to become the best St. Nicholas, Santa Claus, or Mrs. Claus they have the capacity to be. This bond allows the participants to become life-long friends. Laughter and a sense of joy permeate the halls making every minute worthwhile. Every Ho Ho Ho uttered brings a true sense of joy to us all.

It is a difficult dichotomy in the process of trying to be humble and then saying that "I am humble". If true humility exists how is it possible to utter the words "I am humble"? In his letter to the Colossians 2:23 Paul warns: These things indeed have an appearance of wisdom in self-imposed religion, false humility...

Peter in his first letter vs. 5-6: Likewise you younger people, submit yourselves to your elders. Yes, all of you be submissive to one another, and be clothed with humility, for "God resists the proud, But gives grace to the humble. Therefore humble yourselves under the mighty hand of God, that He may exalt you in due time,

We all have a mission. To spread the word, that unto US a child is given (Isaiah 9:6). Also, (Luke 2:10) "Then the angel said to them Do not be afraid, for behold, I bring you good tidings of great joy which will be for ALL people.

All this happens in a setting of peace and tranquility in the world of chaos of suburban Detroit.

In the four years we learned how to have a television presence by experiencing "on the spot" live interview as if we were suddenly faced with a microphone and asked about all the Santas in the world. We learned how to read from a teleprompter as we spread the message of Christmas joy. We learned from the Disney hair and makeup specialist. A Psychologist that had adopted eleven children, helped us learn how to deal with difficult life events including the death of a child and other vulnerable life challenges. We were also blessed by having Karolyn Grimes, who played Zuzu in the film, "It's a Wonderful Life" (it was the 70th anniversary of the movie). We had the benefit of taking acting classes from an accomplished actress from NY city, Catrina Gainey. Catrina Gainey is a gifted and talented actress of color. She provided each of the Santas attending a photograph of her first visit with Santa. He was white, had a fake beard and wig that covered his entire face except for his eyes. She had never seen a white man before, much less a white Santa. The picture depicts the most frightened, wide eyed, black child with the most terrified look. Whenever the Claus encounters a terrified child he recounts the photo to ground him back to the real world.

After attending four different Retreats, the Claus "graduated" and was awarded a medal making him a member of the "Order of St. Nicholas" So far there are less than 10 members from across the country. I am blessed and proud to be a member of this order.

WHY ARE CHILDREN UNDER AGE THREE AFRAID OF SANTA?

There is a very interesting dynamic between young children and Santa. Many Christmas cards and internet photos humorously depict a screaming, crying child that is terrified just being in the presence of Santa.

My observations over the span of several years have helped me draw the following conclusions about the things parents say and do to create the angst with children. In nervous anticipation, some children observe from afar other children bravely sitting on the lap of the big guy in red in the "judgement seat". When it is their turn, panic sets in and completely overwhelms them.

Children are not adults; they do not have the experience to make adult conclusions. They cannot discern what is real and what is make believe. Parents will stand in line with children in tow. Although the children are impatiently misbehaving, the parents talk and the children hear what is being said. Things said include, "look at that Santa", his beard is not real." Or, "look how skinny he is, he can't be real". Something my parents always said was "little pictures have big ears."

Parents will complain about how much time they wasted standing in line waiting so their child can have some time with Santa. These are the same people that tend to complain that Santa did not spend enough time with their child. Parents who are bored or impatient almost always throw the child onto Santa's lap, move away and tell them to say, "cheese". It is then that I will intone the word "Cheeeeeeeeeese" for as long as possible. These and many more factors contribute to the fear and apprehension in the child's experience.

LEGION ARE NOT ONE

Mark 5: 9 "My name is Legion; for we are many." If a child sees more than one Santa in a year, they easily make the determination that they can't all be real. When children see Sponge Bob, they only see one. He never changes. When children have their favorite book read to them the characters never change. The animals on Paw Patrol don't change. Their favorite stuffed animal or dinosaur never change. Yet, parents expect children to see different Santas and determine that they are all real. They aren't. One Santa may have a fake beard or come across as being gruff or mean and another having a real beard and a round belly that shook when he laughed like a bowl full of jelly.

One of my favorite Christmas movies is "The Santa Clause". Santas everywhere are reminded: "In putting on the suit and entering the sleigh, the wearer waives any and all right to any previous identity, real or implied, and fully accepts the duties and responsibilities of Santa Claus, in perpetuity to which some time the wearer becomes unable to do so, by either accident or design." Some Santas take this admonition to heart and some ignore the Clause completely causing children to become anxious. The Claus has often been told about how terrible the last Santa was as he wouldn't even smile!

Well-meaning parents take their children to see three or four or more "Santas" in different venues in the same year. The tell-tale indicator is they will say something like "They were afraid the other day when they saw you, don't you remember?" Or they tell Santa that, "they were afraid last year as well." It is ambitious to think that children remember the brief encounter of a year ago.

People drag their children to different Santas thinking that this one will be different. With this "one" they may get a photo that they will be proud to show their family and friends. A photo showing how well behaved their children are. The un-spoken mirror of reflection of the family is actually, how good they are as parents. Every parent alive thinks their children are the best behaved.

They remind the children of the dreaded "Naughty and Nice List". Parents will remind the children where they rank on the list on that day and at that time. Or they will "sing" "…he knows if you've been bad or good, so be good for goodness sake." Many children are always reminded that they are not acting the way parents have told them to, and so they are reminded that they are bad. Or told they are plain naughty. Or they are told that Santa is going to give them a lump of coal.

I am adding a piece of inside confidential information. Santa hates the role of being the cop for an errant child. Too many parents waste their breath and threaten and cajole their children. "Be good, or else." Then the "or else" often never happens. Santa has watched as a screaming child was thrust into his lap, only to be told to say "cheese" then immediately pulled away in anger because the child did not do as instructed. There was never a chance to create Santa magic. Such a pity!

When I dabbled in managing an art gallery, I learned several things. The first is that the most difficult decision an artist makes in the life of a painting is not deciding on what to paint but to know when the last brush stroke has been made. Perhaps raising children is just like a painting on a piece of canvas that may need one more (or is it two), brush strokes or perhaps one less stroke.

The tongue of the infant clings to the roof of its mouth for thirst; The young children ask for bread, but no one breaks it for them. Lamentations 4:4, But now, O Lord You are our Father, we are the clay and you our potter. And all we are the work of Your hand. Isaiah 64:8.

WINGS AND ROOTS

At times the art of being a parent needs a bit more cultivation. If parents would let children be children, their fears just might go away. Today we expect children to make rational adult decisions. Children two years old are asked if they want to sit in the car seat. Of course, they never want to. Just as children need to be children, adults need to be adults. I am no expert on being a parent and so much has been written about parenting that adults get confused.

Here is what I do know: Somebody has to be the adult in the room. This person or persons need to be there to not only to guide the decision-making process but also to mold the thought processes of children. Children can become more responsible for the actions they choose when they have guidance. We as adults need to discipline ourselves before we attempt to discipline our children.

I have learned a few lessons about dealing with children of all ages. We can only give children two things to help them become as God intended: "Wings and Roots". Wings are first so children can be allowed to fly, Children need to explore and learn from the world around them. They need to be curious, fearful and appreciate with awe the wonder of living. Children need to acquire decision making skills and, at the same time, learn that all decisions have consequences.

Accepting responsibility for the consequences is the major step to being all we can be. Often there are no consequences or accountability for their actions. They raise childern into adulthood who have no idea that doing anything for others is a good thing. Quite often parents blur the definition of what is good. Many parents believe that their childern can do no wrong. And if they somehow do "wrong" then the blame has to belong to someone else. Children would do well to learn how to accept responsibility for their actions and to live with the consequences.

As children naturally mature, they move through periods of seeking their independence. They want to test the limits of the word "no". We as adults need to provide the Roots to let them know they are loved when their choices move them in a direction we would not have chosen for them.

As parents we always want the best for our children and we often have a mistaken belief that we are the providers of all things good as we try to replace the provider of all good things. "My grace is sufficient for you, for My strength is made perfect in weakness." 2 Corinthians 12:9

Do we as parents ever put a wooly-worm into a child's hand without being afraid of it ourselves? Do we as parents show a child how to remove the petals from a daisy using the "she loves me she loves me not" as the petal counter? Do we show children the beauty in different flowers where the bees are gleaning their nectar?

Or are we as parents so wrapped up in the smart phone we constantly play with. Texting now has taken the place of helping children be children. When we encounter a wooly-worm do we quickly pull up a picture and remove the sense of touch and how it tickles when it moves over our fingers? Do we ask Siri or Alexa to show a flower with a bee inside? Smart phones give us information about our world and at the same time take away the real world.

Many People now, watch the world through a very small screen. People record live events instead of watching them unfold right in front of them to "watch them later". When Santa was child he grew up in front of the TV set. What a marvelous babysitter. Now parents are quick to give three year old children their own phones to keep them occupied. Siri is not a babysitter.

THE FEAR FACTOR

The experience of seeing Santa should be a positive experience in every child's life. Personally, I employ a "large" bag of tricks to make that time a positive one with each child. A child in that pre-school age range is not really going to tell Santa what they want for Christmas or any other time. So, the idea at this point is to get a good photo. The key thing is to never force a child to sit in Santa's lap.

Most times I will suggest that the parents hold the child and kind of walk around and not look at Santa. Look at the tree, look at the lights, look at something else. The best results happen when Santa gets up and "photo bombs" the photo before the child knows what is happening.

It is kind of funny when some parents don't want their photo taken with the child. The experience should be about the child. I can assure all parents that when they show the photo to others, that the others don't say "look at that funny blouse you are wearing". "Or, did you know your make up isn't just right". A smiling Santa with a dear precious smiling happy child is the perfect picture. "Utopia!" The thing that helps make magicians successful is the fact that people see what they are used to seeing. People will see the contented child with their parent and Santa in the photo and go ooh and aahh.

From Claus' point of view, it is comforting for small children if Santa sits on the floor and reads or just talks with them from that level. I was at a family party and was told in advance that their 2½ year old girl was terrified of me. We hadn't met yet. Immediately I sat on the floor and read 'Twas the night before Christmas" to all the children. Then each child sat on my legs and told me what they wanted for Christmas. The provided gifts were distributed. The last child was this terrified little girl who spent 15 minutes sitting on the lap of the guy in the red suit. The clincher was when the Claus led the family in singing Happy Birthday to Jesus.

These comments were submitted by Kim.: "Santa Chuck was just a wonderful Santa. He started it off with sitting on the floor with the kids and reading them a story. They were all very scared of him when he got there but by the end of the book, they had all moved in very close. He made the story very funny and the kids were all giggling. My 3 year old daughter has been very scared of Santa this year and wouldn't even look at him at the mall. But after the story he called each kid up by name and gave them a gift and my daughter who wouldn't even look at him at the mall, was sitting on his lap and hugging him by the time he called her name and gave her a present. There was a brother and sister here that were worried Santa didn't know where they lived because they moved and wouldn't even be spending Christmas at their own house this year but at their aunt's house but he reassured them that Santa knew that they were staying there. We left Santa gifts for the kids and we left little notes describing the kids worries and he really helped alleviate their worries. By the end of the party each kid felt very special and knew Santa wouldn't forget them this year. The party was a lot of fun. Santa spent a lot of time with each kid then in turn took any picture we wanted, even pictures with the adults. The party was very special and was a great time. We ended the party with a Happy Birthday Baby Jesus cake. Santa sang Happy Birthday Baby Jesus with the children and then even sat at the table talking with the kids and enjoying cake with them. Everyone loved the party and everyone had a great time including Santa. The adults even said what a wonderful Santa he was."

A NEW LOOK AT THE DREADED "NAUGHTY AND NICE LIST"

Santa's chair no matter how it is decorated always reminded me of the "judgement" seat. Probably because of my upbringing in Roman Catholic school system complete with Sister Mary Sadistic. For years, the Claus, has made and used a "Naughty Nice" list as a tool. It was used by this guilty human into the self-proclaimed position of being the judge of good and bad behavior in children. The Claus used a theatrical device that instantly displayed a list that only Santa could read.

My entire Santa persona would hinge on the "N&N List". It was meant only to be a tool to promote being good, most children knew they fell short of being good. And if they didn't, they were reminded constantly about being naughty. It has also allowed me to realize that children very often are severely traumatized by the very suggestion of the N&N list. The fear of a penalty for a mistake looms large.

The introspection has helped my faith journey and has moved me closer to trusting the bible in my "Santa life". The more that I have read in the bible the more I have learned that I am not the judge. Matthew 7:1-2 has the message, Judge not, that you be not judged. For with what judgement you judge, you will be judged; and with the measure you use, it will be measured to you. Luke 6:37 echoes by saying Judge not, and you shall not be judged. Condemn not, and you will not be condemned, Forgive and you will be forgiven. Romans 3:23 "for all have sinned and fall short of the glory of God. And James 2:13: gives us the icing on the cake. …Mercy triumphs over judgement. These verses provided a maturity level to understand that as Santa I had it all wrong!

Many people still cling to ideas of right and wrong. We live in a period of time when moral relativism tends to change the view. We as parents have gotten lax about teaching right and wrong. Our adult children have followed suit quit teaching right and wrong and now we are into our third generation of people using the mantra: "if it feels good do it." This thinking has gotten many a public figure into more trouble than they could handle.

SO, HERE IS THE PROBLEM

How do I (as the arbiter of good and bad, the one who decides the naughty and the nice, the one who determines if a lump of coal or a gift is to be given for each child), teach children I know they have not been good but I love them anyway? I don't like what they may have done but I still love them. They are getting a gift because they believe in the giver of that Gift, indeed Santa loves them. How do I teach them in a two minute visit about grace when they know nothing of God's love?

How do I teach them that they do not have to do anything to receive their free gift from Santa? Just accept and believe in the giver? Just as we do not have to do anything to be given the gift of eternal salvation, but, confess our sins, ask for forgiveness and believe in Jesus the Christ. My entire focus has changed. Isn't that just like being a Christian? Should they/we somehow be held accountable to receive the gift? Yes we should! But our belief in Jesus as the Christ allows us to be sure that the price has been paid.

For you were bought at a price. 1 Corinthians 6:20

If I ask children if they have been good, ninety nine percent will say, "yes, they have been good". When asked if they are ever bad, perhaps fifteen percent will reply yes or maybe hedge their bets and admit to being bad sometimes. Needing to change my focus perhaps asking a different question might be in order. Something like "What can you do to help your Mom and Dad?" Or is there anything you can do to stop fighting with your brothers or sisters?

When I ask about their brothers or sisters I always get an earful. Siblings tend to bicker, quibble, or outright fight with each other. When I ask if they ever fight with their siblings, I am told "of course not" or some other similar statement. I tell them that Santa does not like it when they fight with their siblings and try to have them buy into the thought that there could be one day per week when they don't fight. Parents think "that will never happen".

I empower the children to choose the day they will not fight with their siblings. Once I allowed the youngest one of three brothers to pick a day before Christmas Eve that he would not fight with his brothers. The day was picked and he made every effort to stay at Grandma's house so he would not fight. His mother said that they all prepared for that day, circled it on the calendar. They actually went the entire day without fighting. The implication was that Santa needed to see a day circled or crossed with an X or he might not come on Christmas Eve.

While being the Claus at a local restaurant I sat at the table with a nine year old boy and his two sisters ages 14 and 15. Determining that yes, indeed, they sometimes fought (what a surprise!) I challenged them as a family to not fight at all for three days before Christmas. They could pick the days but I needed to see three "Xs" on the calendar; otherwise I would think twice about stopping at their home on Christmas Eve. They all agreed that my request was impossible; they didn't think they could do it. During the next hour they had a family discussion. I surmised that they were talking about the food in front of them and their day at school. As they were leaving, I was given a crayon colored picture of Santa with the words "Family Challenge Accepted" written in crayon on which each one wrote their name to seal the deal. Magic!

My daughter has suggested that instead of talking about good and bad, I should ask: "what are they doing to not fight with siblings and friends." That actually was the catalyst for my change of focus this past year and from now on. "WOW!" Santa Magic from within the family.

THEY ARE SO WITTY

Technology has made it difficult to keep up with the increasingly knowledgeable children of today. Smart phones and the instant access of the internet makes matching wits a wonderful opportunity to test the old Santa brain. The Claus jokes all the time about having a VCR that continues to flash 12:00 noon while listening to music on something called a phonograph.

One would think that "there's an APP for that" would replace the necessity of having a Santa "meet and greet" and create magic with children of all ages. Apps might make a child smile, but the odds are against it. How satisfying can it be to have a computer voice say "Hi Don George, how are you today?" Compared to a real life jovial person sincerely interested in creating joy and magic.

Technical devices give us information and it has been said that information is power. But alas, information is not communication.

Children as young as six are questioning the existence of Santa Claus thanks to siblings and classmates that tell them otherwise. My challenge to prove Santa is "real" increases every year and it is important to come up with new gimmicks to increase the wow factor.

Eight and nine year-old children question Santa a lot and getting to outsmart them is a most wonderful challenge. If you can't dazzle them with brilliance, baffle them with old fashioned wit and Santa Magic.

THE MAGIC
REVISITED

BRIGHTER LIGHTS
LOUDER SIRENS

Several times the Claus has been honored to be on a fire truck as part of a parade. Parades require planning or Santa arrives to a crowd of 40 people. Three times the parade planners in a nearby town and they did it right. Notices in the newspaper, print ads and an exemplary job by the radio and TV station plus the Chamber of Commerce promoting the coming of Santa, allowed 3,000 people to be downtown. As we turned the corner, with lights on, sirens on, and being mobbed by a sea of people gave me the feeling of being a rock star.

The procession to the "chair" in the park had a rock star feel, shaking hands, giving autographs as "Santa Chuck" surely makes one feel very good. The parade was over at 11:45 and people were lined up to visit with Santa until after three in the afternoon. The cable company that promoted the event was ready to shut down at the agreed time of 2:00, but they stayed another hour. Still there were about 100 children were left in the lurch not being able to visit Santa in the park in their downtown. The Claus felt very bad and vowed to never let that happen again. The next year the Claus remained until every child was seen.

For the first event at this location it was unseasonably warm and for the most part people were comfortable wearing light jackets. The second event a year later the reverse was true. It was cold and even "layers" didn't seem to keep people warm. Several times Santa had to tell the elves and other helpers to seek the warmth of the shop across the street offering warmth and free hot chocolate. Even though it was bitter cold, every child was seen by Santa. Magic!

The third city brings Santa at the end of the Halloween parade. There are questions about rushing the season, But what the heck everyone else does. HO HO HO!

CULTURE SHOCK PART 1

The Claus was invited to be the guest at a 630 unit apartment building in beautiful downtown Pittsburgh. The location was the closest building to the arena the Pittsburgh Penguins call home.

Santa lives in a small town and needs to step into the real world on occasion. It was a BYOB social event allowing residents at that address to share some fellowship, have a beverage of their choice, with a Santa photo op. Over the course of the evening a diverse cross section of the melting pot of America was on display. Seventy-five people ventured down to the social area and had a good time.

People of many ethnic cultures and occupations attended the event. It became a bit overwhelming to know that many people attending did not have the same understanding of Christmas that Christians have. There were people born in America and many having a different heritage. I spent several minutes communicating with a man from India. We talked about his belief in the supreme being and my concept of God. After having seen "The Story of God" series on the National Geographic network with host Morgan Freeman, I was empowered to ask and learn. At the end of our conversation he concluded with the phrase, "I wish you peace in your journey and Have a Merry Christmas."

It was a relief that no one there objected to Santa saying "Merry Christmas". I met with Doctors and Lawyers and Professors and Students and so many other people from all walks of life. For the most part these people worked with their minds to help make life better for all of humankind. Having them together created magic.

CULTURE SHOCK PART 2

One day after the tour of urban ethnicity I was immersed in a very rural setting at an event sponsored by a local Historical Society. Sixty people from a farming community gathered at the Grange hall to celebrate their commonality as well as the joys and heartaches of the past year. Many people had been devastated by local flooding that had destroyed over 30 homes. For the most part these people worked with their hands to make a living. They came to eat a meal with their families and friends. They came to celebrate Christmas by way of a party. They came to celebrate the joy of giving (and taking).

Like most events it was a make it up as you go program. My directions to get there said it is the big building by the fair grounds. The big building had several pick-up trucks parked in front so I took a shot. I determined It was the right place as I peeked through a crack in the door and saw several people that I knew. They had the party at a different venue last year, but, this was the place. The participants were in a festive mood. The Claus bursting into the room made it feel more like Christmas. They all were fed and now let's have some fun! The Claus for the evening was Alex Trebek. The winning question to the answer was Martin Luther, with Who is credited with being the first to decorate indoor Christmas trees?

Each year we conduct a naughty Santa's gift exchange. Kind of like let's take not make a deal. Door number 1 or door number 2, this gift or that gift you choose but then someone has the same option. For 45 minutes unopened gifts were claimed and lost as they were claimed by someone else. The laughter reached a fevered pitch. Magic! Different location, same magic!

CULTURE SHOCK PART 3

The Claus was the star attraction in a photo shoot at the studio of a local photographer. The event was to benefit the local women's homeless shelter. For these special photos of their child(ren), parents "paid" with a specific gift requested by a shelter resident. We each had our tasks with the photographer leading the caravan comprised of four vehicles loaded with twelve helpers. Santa's task was to distribute these gifts to people who had lost everything but the clothes on their backs. It was very emotional and tears of gratitude and humility almost flooded the facility. The most gratifying magic was created!

On the same night, The Claus was the invited guest at a home in a very elite neighborhood. The house was huge and full of guests and, to Santa's delight, included over 90 children. I think it is a fair guess to say that none of the children were lacking for anything. They possessed an entitlement mentality for the wrong reasons. They wanted more because they had more already. There was no display of gratitude. There were no tears There was no joy. What a shame!

KNEELING AT THE KING'S THRONE

I wonder if anyone ever considered the composition or make up of a throne? Is the throne a big giant chair in which judgement is passed down to the peons? Is the throne where only the king sits? Is the throne that gold plated ornate chair where it can be said "off with their heads" if someone dares to even touch it? Is it a movie prop?

Or can it be something less luxurious? Is it possible that a throne can be simple? Is a throne always to pass judgement or can it be where mercy is handed out. Can it be made of rough boards and filled with straw to feed animals? It takes foresight or vision or hindsight to know that the manger in a cattle stall held a king.

Foresight: "For unto us a child is born, unto us a son is given: and the government shall be upon his shoulder: and his name shall be called Wonderful, Counsellor, The mighty God, The everlasting Father, The Prince of Peace." (Isaiah 9-6).

"Now gather yourself in troops, O daughter of troops; He has laid siege against us; They will strike the judge of Israel with a rod on the cheek. But you, Bethlehem Ephrathah, Though you are little among the thousands of Judah, Yet out of you shall come forth to Me The One to be Ruler in Israel, Whose goings forth are from of old, From everlasting." (Micah 5:1-2)

Vision: "And she brought forth her firstborn Son, and wrapped Him in swaddling cloths, and laid Him in a manger, because there was no room for them in the inn. Now there were in the same country shepherds living out in the fields, keeping watch over their flock by night. And behold an angel of the Lord stood before them, and the glory of the Lord shone around them, and they were greatly afraid. Then the angel said to them, 'Do not be afraid, for behold, I bring you good tidings of great joy which will be to all people. For there is born to you this day in the city of David a Savior, who is Christ the Lord. And this will be the sign to you: You will find a Babe wrapped in swaddling cloths, lying in a manger. And suddenly there was with the angel a multitude of the heavenly host praising God and saying: 'Glory to God in the highest, and on earth peace, goodwill toward men!' So, it was, when the angels had gone away from them into heaven, that the shepherds said to one another, "Let us now go to Bethlehem and see this thing that has come to pass, which the Lord has made known to us. And they came with haste and found Mary and Joseph, and the Babe lying in a manger. Now when they had seen Him, they made widely known the saying which was told them concerning this Child. And all those who heard it marveled at those things which were told them by the shepherds. (Luke 2:2-17)

Hindsight comes from the verse following the most Quoted verse in the bible: "For God so loved the world that He gave His only begotten Son, that whoever believes in Him should not perish but have everlasting life. For God, did not send His Son into the world to condemn the world, but that the world through Him might be saved." (John 3:16-17).

When the President of the United States boards a plane, any plane, that plane instantly is designated as "Air Force One. " Any location where Jesus the Christ is, he is on the throne. It becomes "King Force One" Two centuries later we have the benefit of all three: Foresight, Vision, and Hindsight. The manger becomes the throne. And this is where I kneel.

Santa is not the reason for the season. Nor are snow, snowmen, penguins or silver bells. Jesus Christ, the King of Kings is the reason and it is for that very reason He deserves all homage that I can give. As John the Baptist is quoted in the Gospel of St. John, "I must decrease so He can increase". And so it is… Santa is very relevant until midnight on Christmas Eve… coincidently the same time many Christians celebrate the birth of Jesus. Santa must decrease so He can increase.

THE CLAUS THROUGH THE LENS OF A CAMERA

When an event is over, it easy to say, "yeah, I thought it went well." But it is much better to see the event through the eyes of others. It has been said that in many cultures taking someone's photo was forbidden because people were convinced that with each photo their souls were lost. There have been thousands of photos taken of Santa Chuck. I am here to say that I haven't lost my soul but have found it and it is bigger and better than ever before.

From Stephanie: "Santa Chuck was our Santa Claus for our event today. He arrived early and was ready to go. I cannot say enough about how wonderfully he interacted with the children. He posed for photos with the kids while sitting in the chair and walked around the room to give the kids time to adjust to his presence. He also positioned himself in the background for children that were too afraid because of their age to sit on his lap. We were able to get photos of each and every child with him today. Even some kids that were afraid initially went to him to talk before they left. He also brought books with him to share story time which the kids loved. I can't image having anyone else for my future Santa events."

From Rebecca: Santa Chuck (aka. Nick the Claus) made our event truly magical. He took the time to make each and every child comfortable with him, even learning small details before greeting them to be sure they felt connected immediately. Never once breaking character, even the adults left feeling the magic of the holiday season in their hearts after chatting with the Claus. I look forward to a long standing relationship with Santa Chuck for years to come as our event continues to evolve. Thank you for your touch of magic.

Santa Chuck, aka. Nick the Claus humbly and gratefully says Thank You, Merry Christmas to all, and to all a good night. My magical journey continues.

ENLIGHTENMENT FROM AN ORIGINAL AND PERHAPS THE BEST

On The Meaning of Christmas:

Oh, Christmas isn't just a day. It is a frame of mind... and that is what has been changing. That is why I'm glad I'm here. Maybe I can do something about it.

Kirs Kringle, Miracle on 34th Street

CPSIA information can be obtained
at www.ICGtesting.com
Printed in the USA
BVHW072024131119
563792BV00001B/2/P